How to Spot Errors (X) & Improve the Sentences

By **SC Gupta** & **Kumkum Gupta**
The renowned & versatile author-duo of books to master the English Language

arihant
Inspiring Minds
Arihant Publications (I) Pvt Ltd, Meerut

Delhi Office: 4577/15, Ramchhaya, Agarwal Road, Darya Ganj, New Delhi - 2
Phone : 011-23280316, 47630600 ; Fax : 011-43540876

Head Office : Kalindi, TP Nagar, Meerut, Phone : 0121-2401479, 2512970, 2402029 ;
Fax : 0121-2401648, Email : info@arihantbooks.com

Zonal & Regional Offices :

North Zone — **Agra**: 8/195, New Engineers' Colony, Kaushalpur, Agra, Ph. 0562 – 6451531, Email: arihant_agra02@yahoo.co.in **Delhi–1 (for Delhi & NCR) :** 4577/15, Ramchhaya, Agarwal Road, Darya Ganj, New Delhi – 110002, Ph. 011 – 23280316, Fax. 011 – 43540876, Email: arihant_delhi07@yahoo.co.in; **Delhi–2 (for Haryana, Himachal, J&K & Punjab) :** 4577/15, Ramchhaya, Agarwal Road, Darya Ganj, New Delhi – 110002, Ph. 011 – 23280316, Fax. 011 – 43540876, Email: arihant_delhi07@yahoo.co.in **Jaipur**: C–8, Link Road, Jalupura MD Road, Near Hotel Apoorva, Jaipur – 302 001 (Raj), Ph. 0141 – 4033077, Email : deepmahur85@gmail.com; **Kota**: 5-J-18, Talwardi, Behind T.T. Hospital, Kota–324009 (Rajasthan.), 0744–2406760, Email : arihant_kota@yahoo.co.in; **Lucknow**: C – 22,Vijay Laxmi Transport Building, Transport Nagar, Kanpur Road, Lucknow – 226 012 (UP), Ph. 0522 – 6459009, Fax : 0522-4028575, Email : arihant_lko@yahoo.com; **Haldwani**: Raja Enterprises, Varun Complex, Rampur Road, Haldwani (Uttarakhand), Ph. 05946 – 235456 ; Email : arihant_kashipur@yahoo.co.in; **Meerut**: Kalindi, TP Nagar, Meerut, Ph: 0121-6534323, Email: arihant_meerutbranch@yahoo.co.in.

East Zone — **Bhubaneshwar**: 14, Shahid Nagar, Bhubaneshwar – 751007 (Orissa), Ph. 064 – 2503050, 09938211103, Email : bhubaneshwar@arihantbooks.com; **Kolkata**: 4, Tottee Lane, Kolkata – 700016 (WB), Ph. 033 – 22526713, Fax. 033 – 22523564, Email: arihant_kol@yahoo.co.in; **Guwahati**: Aastha Towers, Ist Floor, Module No. XIII, CK Road, Pan Bazar, Guwahati – 781 001, (Asom) Ph. 0361 – 2731599, E-mail : arihant_guwahati@yahoo.co.in; **Patna**: Gangotri Complex, U/465, Lohia Nagar, Kankarbagh, Patna – 20 (Bihar), Ph. 0612 – 2360623, Email: cafpatna@rediffmail.com.

Central Zone — **Nagpur**: 27, Nathuji Pise Complex, Opp. Mokshadham, New Gate, Beside Hanuman Mandir, Great Nag Road, Nagpur – 14, (Maharashtra), Ph. 0712 – 2748211 ; Email : arihant_nagpur1@yahoo.co.in.

South Zone — **Hyderabad**: Plot No.–115, SBI Colony, Kavadiguda, Near Sri Satya Sai Temple, Hyderabad–500020, Ph. 040 – 65347774, 66107772, Email: hyd.arihant@gmail.com; **Bengaluru**: 362, 10th Main, 2nd Cross, Ist Block, Basaveshwara Nagar, Bengaluru-560079, Mob : +919242693192

Price : Rs 75.00

PO No. : TXT-59-T052389-3-23

Laser Typesetting : Arihant Prakashan DTP Unit, Meerut

Printed & Bound in India
by Arihant Publications (India) Limited

For further information on
Arihant Group, log in : www.arihantbooks.com

Preface

This is a very important book for the students who are taking various competitive examinations to achieve some important avenues in their life. In most of the competitive examinations, you find ten questions relating to Spotting the Errors and five or ten questions relating to Phrase Substitution in the question paper of English language. There are 108 exercises of Spotting the Errors along with their answers with justification and 32 exercises of phrase Substitution, in this book.

There is no shortcut of solving such type of questions. One must learn grammar rules and their correct usage as well as various grammatical concepts and notions well. One should also cover various exceptions in respect to various grammatical rules. Learning about the unenglish expressions and superfluous use of various words will also help you in solving such questions. Candidates should also understand it well that mere cramming the various grammatical rules will not help them in solving such questions, they must practice again and again.

Wish you best of luck!

Authors
129-South West Block,
Near Eidgah
Alwar (Rajasthan)
Tel-(0144) 2700438

Contents

Spotting Errors

How to Solve such Questions?

In most of the competitive examinations, the question paper of English contains questions relating to spotting errors: A given sentence is usually divided in four or five parts marked A to E. Last option refers to 'No error'. The candidate is required to find out the part having an error. The error may be relating to the use of; article, preposition, tense, verb, noun, pronoun, adverb, adjective, conjunction, subject-verb agreement, etc. Sometimes, the error may also be that of unenglish expressions or superfluous use of some word.

*Please note that there is no 'shortcut' of answering these questions. You should have good command over grammar rules and their usage. **First learn the rules and** then attempt these questions, see the answer and find the error. **The more you practise, the more confidence you get.** Just cramming the rules will not solve your problem. Solve the exercises again and again, you will surely find improvement in your scoring.*

Good knowledge of grammatical rules and their correct usage in proper perspective is the only way of scoring good marks in all types of questions relating to errors.

ARTICLES

Directions : *Read each sentence to find out whether there is any error in it. The error, if any, will be in one part of the sentence. The number of that part is the answer. If there is no error, then the answer is last option.*

Exercise 1

1. We (A)/saw (B)/a elephant (C)/ in the zoo (D)/No error (E).
2. It is (A)/a most (B)/beautiful (C)/painting of the gallery (D)/No error (E).
3. Mr. Gaurav Sharma (A)/is (B)/coming to (C)/dinner (D)/No error (E).
4. I (A)/go (B)/to cinema (C)/every sunday (D)/No error (E).
5. He (A)/ went there (B)/a hour (C)/ago (D)/No error (E).
6. He (A)/always speaks (B)/truth (C)/No error (D).
7. Kashmiri (A)/shawls (B)/are made of (C)/the hair of sheep (D)/No error (E).
8. The Taj mahal (A)/is (B)/situated (C)/at the Agra (D)/No error (E).
9. Bible (A)/said that (B)/the sun (C)/goes round the earth (D)/No error (E).
10. An horse(A)/is (B)/running(C)/in the ground (D)/No error(E).

Exercise 2

1. An European (A)/dish (B)/is (C)/very famous (D)/No error (E).
2. Rome (A)/was (B)/not built (C)/in a day (D)/No error (E).
3. Ritika (A)/helps (B)/poor and (C)/the sick people (D)/No error (E).
4. The Sapna (A)/is a very (B)/beautiful (C)/girl (D)/No error (E).
5. I (A)/saw (B)/an one rupee note (C)/on the road (D)/No error (E).
6. The boy (A)/is (B)/swimming (C)/in the pool (D)/No error (E).
7. Here is a red (A)/shirt (B)/which Sapna gave me (C)/yesterday (D)/ No error (E).
8. Shatabdi express (A)/runs (B)/very (C)/fast (D)/No error (E).
9. Parul (A)/was also invited (B)/to the lunch hosted by the queen, (C)/at her cottage yesterday (D)/No error (E).
10. My uncle (A)/is (B)/a (C)/S.P. (D)/No error (E).

Exercise 3

1. Gold (A)/is (B)/an useful (C)/metal (D)/No error (E).
2. This is (A)/a good dress (B)/but (C)/that's a better one (D)/No error (E).
3. Rupam (A)/presented me (B)/a ring (C)/The ring is lost (D)/No error (E).
4. The Punjabi (A)/is (B)/a sweet language (C)/of Punjab (D)/No error (E).

5. Adnan Sami (A)/is the (B)/most popular (C)/singer in Indian film industry (D)/ No error (E).
6. The sun (A)/rises (B)/in (C)/east (D)/No error (E).
7. The teaching (A)/profession (B)/is (C)/good for women (D)/No error (E).
8. The milk (A)/is (B)/good (C)/for health (D)/No error (E).
9. I (A)/think (B)/a baby (C)/is crying (D)/No error (E).
10. Kunal (A)/was (B)/sent to (C)/a prison (D)/No error (E).

Exercise 4

1. I (A)/will go (B)/there (C)/by train or bus (D)/No error (E).
2. My parents (A)/sometimes (B)/comes to school (C)/to see the Principal (D)/No error (E).
3. Riya (A)/went home (B)/very late (C)/last Monday (D)/No error (E).
4. The winters (A)/are (B)/generally very (C)/cold here (D)/No error (E).
5. The monkeys (A)/jump (B)/on (C)/the trees (D)/No error (E).
6. The dog (A)/is (B)/a (C)/faithful animal (D)/No error (E).
7. Chief Minister (A)/will (B)/decide (C)/the matter (D)/No error (E).
8. Kshitiz (A)/is (B)/a (C)/honest boy (D)/No error (E).
9. The sun (A)/rises in (B)/the east (C)/is an universal truth (D)/No error (E).
10. Times of India (A)/is a most popular (B)/news paper (C)/of these days (D)/No error (E).

Exercise 5

1. Three children (A)/died (B)/in a (C)/bus accident yesterday (D)/No error (E).
2. The Mahatma Gandhi (A)/was (B)/also called (C)/'Bapu' (D)/No error (E).
3. Chinese (A)/are (B)/fond of (C)/chowmin (D)/No error (E).
4. Taj Mahal (A)/is a (B)/beautiful (C)/building in Agra (D)/No error (E).
5. The capital (A)/of (B)/UK is (C)/London (D)/No error (E).
6. My mother (A)/is cooking (B)/in a (C)/kitchen (D)/No error (E).
7. The teacher (A)/called a (B)/last boy (C)/standing in the queue (D)/No error (E).
8. The apple (A)/a day (B)/keeps (C)/the doctors away (D)/ No error (E).
9. The more (A)/I learn history (B)/the more(C)/I get bored (D)/No error (E).
10. The intelligent (A)/should (B)/help (C)/the duffer (D)/No error (E).
11. Shreya (A)/gave(B)/me (C)/the watch (D)/No error (E).

Exercise 6

1. In the conclusion it (A)/may be said (B)/that the writer has surpassed (C)/the ethical norms (D).
2. It is the most(A)/important point that(B)/you have to(C)/understand well (D).
3. He said to me(A),/"I think you (B)/will never (C)/turn a traitor (D)".
4. Ramesh told me (A)/that he first went (B)/to the Mexico and (C)/then to the Netherlands (D).
5. My mother forbade (A)/my sister to (B)/go to theatre (C)/at night (D).
6. One should be true (A)/to one's words in (B)/order to earn good name (C)/and fame in the life (D).
7. I have been waiting (A)/for her (B)/for more than (C)/half a hour (D).
8. You should not spend (A)/good part of the day (B)/in gossiping and wandering (C)/here and there (D).
9. Will you please (A)/give me (B)/little milk (C)/for my cat (D)?
10. He informed me (A)/that he had gone (B)/to the church (C)/to offer prayers (D).

TRANSLATION AND TENSE

Exercise 7

1. I have come to (A)/know that (B)/his father has died (C)/three days ago (D).
2. When will you find (A)/out a solution (B)/to this problem (C),/you will be awarded a prize (D).
3. Before the alarm had stopped (A)/ringing (B)/Nisha had telephoned (C)/the police (D).
4. This is (A)/the first time (B)/that I see such (C)/an interesting movie (D).
5. Whenever he is coming (A)/here, he brings (B)/many (C)/gifts for me (D).
6. Now a days (A)/he teaches English (B)/because the teacher of English (C)/has gone for a month's leave (D).
7. "It is high time (A)/you are starting (B)/this business" (C)/said Ram to Mahesh (D).
8. I will let you know (A)/as soon as I (B)/will get (C)/any news in this regard (D).
9. When I will (A)/cross fifty, my (B)/wife will cross (C)/forty five (D).
10. The secret of his good health (A)/lies in the fact (B)/that he is getting up early (C)/and goes to bed early (D).

Exercise 8

1. The students sitting on the dais (A),/studied here (B)/for three years, but (C)/they have never created any problem (D)
2. A philogynist is a person (A)/who loves woman (B)/but a mysogynist is a person (C)/who is hating woman (D).
3. It is appearing to me (A)/that you are (B)/trying to destabilise (C)/the present committee (D).
4. I have been knowing her (A)/for many years (B)/but I don't know (C)/where she works (D).
5. If he would have done this (A),/he would have done wrong (B)/and would have deceived (C)/many of his relatives (D).
6. The victim tried to tell us (A)/what has happened (B)/but his words (C)/were not audible (D).
7. I want you to (A)/pick up the box of eggs gently (B)/and kept it in (C)/the corner carefully (D). ***(Bank of Baroda PO)***
8. She came to (A)/the party much (B)/later than (C)/I expect (D).
9. I lived here (A)/for five years (B),/so I know about the (C)/problems of this colony (D).
10. The chairman had not taken (A)/any decision until (B)/he had studied (C)/the case thoroughly (D).
11. They got everything (A)/ready for the visitors (B)/long before (C)/they reached there (D).
12. He switched on (A)/the light before (B)/he entered (C)/the room (D)/No error (E).
13. I have been admiring (A)/her for the (B)/voice with which (C)/she is gifted (D).
14. He was with me (A)/uptil now (B),/so don't (C)/punish him for the delay (D).
15. Several survey reports (A)/indicate that (B)/the number of (C)/drug addicts is grown gradually (D).
16. 'Here is coming up Bachchan!' (A)/, said he (B)/when he was (C)/waiting for him (D).
17. I could not recall (A)/when she has told me (B)/about her (C)/affair with Gopal (D).
18. Four and four (A)/always made eight (B)/cannot (C)/be questioned by anyone (D).
19. She hopes to (A)/become an engineer (B)/after she will complete (C)/her education (D).

TENSE

Exercise 9

1. When you will find (A)/a solution to this problem (B)/you will be able (C)/to get this project (D).
2. The teacher told us (A)/that we should remain (B)/in the hostel (C)/if it rains (D).
3. I could not recall (A)/what she has advised me (B)/in this matter (C).
4. By this time tomorrow (A)/she has had reached (B)/there positively (C).
5. I will inform (A)/you as soon as (B)/I will get any news (C)/about his health (D).
6. A recent survey (A)/indicates (B)/that the number of drug addicts (C)/grew day by day (D).
7. Before the alarm (A)/had stopped ringing (B)/Reena had pulled up the shade (C).
8. If I was you (A)/I would have told (B)/the Principal (C)/to keep his mouth shut (D).
9. I want you (A)/to pick up the box (B)/of glasses gently (C)/and kept it on the table carefully (D).
10. The victim tried (A)/to tell us what has happened (B)/but his words (C)/were not audible (D).

NOUN

Exercise 10

1. He acted not (A)/as per my advice (B)/but somebody else (C).
2. Pakistan's problems (A)/are also as (B)/serious as (C)/that of India (D).
3. When I reached (A)/at the gate of his (B)/house I found his (C)/locking up the gate (D).
4. Many of the question (A)/appeared in this question paper (B)/are too difficult (C)/to solve (D).
5. I visited (A)/Ram's and Sita's house (B)/and found the couple missing (C).
6. All the girls students (A)/are advised to (B)/attend the meeting positively (C).
7. She gave me (A)/two important informations (B)/I had been waiting for (C)/the last two months (D).
8. The English teacher (A)/gave him a home work (B)/to complete that (C)/by night positively (D).
9. She could not complete (A)/even the two third (B)/of the book (C)/owing to her busy schedule (D).

10. All the woman teachers (A)/are agitating (B)/against the haughty attitude (C)/of the Principal (D).

11. He informed that (A)/he had lost a packet (B)/of the hundred (C)/rupees notes (D).

12. He has ordered (A)/bricks for the proposed (B)/shopping complex (C).

13. She has ordered (A)/two dozens of copies (B)/of English book by Mr. Gupta (C).

14. She uses a good (A)/quality of shampoo (B)/so her hairs are (C)/black (D).

15. I known nothing (A)/about her (B)/where about (C).

PRONOUNS

Exercise 11

1. The board of directors (A)/want the facilities (B)/of car and accommodation (C)/for itself (D).
2. Every teacher (A)/and every student (B)/of this school is determined to do their best (C)/for the benefit of all (D).
3. The officer (A)/as well as the (B)/clerks absented themselves (C)/from the office (D).
4. There were (A)/five active workers (B)/and three lazy one (C)/in the factory (D).
5. There is none (A)/who can support you (B)/in this crucial period (C).
6. Any of the (A)/two photos which reflect (B)/the natural beauty of Kashmir (C)/is worth seeing (D).
7. The guests (A)/whom we were talking (B)/about have arrived (C)/are my relatives (D).
8. He introduced (A)/to the chairman as (B)/the president of the (C)/workers association (D).
9. As a student (A)/of arts (B)/you are much better (C)/than him (D).
10. He hates everybody (A)/and everything who (B)/reminds him (C)/of his blunder (D).

Exercise 12

1. Whomever (A)/does not come in time (B)/will not be allowed (C)/to mark his presence (D).
2. The six partners (A)/are at daggers drawn (B)/so they do not talk (C)/to each other (D).
3. If someone has (A)/completed the work (B)/he may leave (C).
4. She lent me (A)/some money with the condition (B)/that I should return (C)/the same within a month (D).

5. The teacher instructed (A)/the peon to let (B)/the students and I (C) /go into the office of Principal (D).
6. The candidate (A)/being a commerce graduate (B)/she is eligible (C)/for the post of accountant (D).
7. In all circumstances (A)/I have helped him (B)/and he knows (C).
8. I don't appreciate (A)/him who laugh (B)/at others without (C)/any reason (D).
9. You and myself (A)/will enjoy the function (B)/being arranged in honour of (C)/ the new Principal (D).
10. He asked for (A)/permission to go to the cinema (B)/but his mother (C)/did not give (D).

INFINITIVE-PARTICIPLES

Exercise 13

1. Being often ill (A)/and frequently absent (B)/she had no opportunity to complete his work (C)/or do much of it in toto (D).
2. Taking breakfast (A)/he went to the office (B)/and ordered the staff (C)/to complete the work without any further delay (D).
3. Without taking proper care (A)/the doctors would (B)/not have been saved (C)/ the life of this patient (D).
4. Going towards the gate (A)/with a cup of tea (B)/somebody switched off (C)/the light (D).
5. He does nothing (A)/but to find faults (B)/with others (C)/and laugh at them (D).
6. The Chief Minister (A)/should not let (B)/the terrorist activities (C)/to grow in our state (D).
7. Many persons are coming (A)/to his concert (B)/to hear him to sing (C)/the religious songs (D).
8. Having had reached (A)/the station, you (B)/may make a telephone (C)/to your boss (D).
9. It is better to stay (A)/at home than to go to market (B)/when it is raining (C).
10. He asked me to (A)/completely forget her (B)/but only I know it is not possible (C).

PREPOSITIONS

Exercise 14

1. He was sleeping (A)/in his room when a thief (B)/entered into his house (C)/and took away a lot of things (D).
2. In her concluding speech (A)/she said almost nothing (B)/worth listening to (C).

3. It was apparent for (A)/everyone present (B)/that if the patient did not receive (C)/immediate medical aid he would die (D).
4. He proposed me (A)/that we should go to the Disco (B)/and then have (C)/dinner at a restra (D).
5. There appears (A)/to be a little laison (B)/among the (C)/two groups of the society (D).
6. The team (A)/complained to the manager (B)/against the captain (C)/and the poor facilities provided in the hotel (D).
7. Yesterday I met (A)/a man (B)/who was blind with the right eye (C).
8. The principal distributed (A)/the sweet among our friends (B)/who bade him farewell (C).
9. As per the invitation care (A)/Rahim marries with Sayra (B)/on 13th December Monday (C).
10. The debacle of the congress party (A)/admit no other explanation (B)/than its (C)/poor performance during the last five years (D).

Exercise 15

1. The society does not (A)/hold itself responsible (B)/for the loss or damage to (C)/any item (D).
2. In spite of being (A)/very busy at project work (B)/he saves time (C)/to the relatives (D).
3. Some persons (A)/get promotions (B)/even if they are not (C)/worthy for them (D).
4. While he was returning (A)/from the office (B)/a man attacked on (C)/him with a dagger (D).
5. The decline of her moral (A)/was caused by a lot of (B)/factors that were once (C)/fascinating to her (D).
6. He took me to a restra (A)/and ordered for two cups (B)/of cold coffee (C)/which the waiter brought in an hour (D).
7. There are some animals (A)/that can live both in water and land (B)/ without any difficulty (C).
8. During his tour (A)/to the south (B)/he visited not only to Madras (C)/but also Karnataka (D).
9. The President Mr. Kalam (A)/is much sought after (B)/by school students and (C)/is invited for many functions (D).
10. His mother is not well (A)/but he (B)/does not look for her (C)/properly (D).

Exercise 16

1. We may have to await for (A)/a new political revival (B)/to eradicate the (C)/corruption from our economy (D).
2. When she was (A)/in jail (B)/she was debarred to send (C)/a letter even to her son (D).
3. Despite of the best efforts (A)/put by the doctors (B)/the condition of the patient (C)/is deteriorating from bad to worse (D).
4. The militant yielded for (A)/the temptation and fell (B)/into the trap (C)/of police (D).
5. Many people in India (A)/are dying from hunger (B)/but government seems (C)/to be ignorant of such crude fact (D).
6. In difficult time (A)/she prefers keeping her counsel (B)/rather than wandering (C)/here and there for relief (D).
7. The persons who are (A)/suffering from diabetes are (B)/advised to substitute (C)/saccharine by sugar (D).
8. He always says (A)/that he prefers to go (B)/home to stay in (C)/a hotel at night (D).
9. Hardly had we settled down (A)/for the rest (B)/when we were startled by the (C)/strange sound of trumpets (D).
10. He was able to (A)/free himself with (B)/the debts by (C)/working day and night (D).

CONJUNCTIONS

Exercise 17

1. She was not (A)/so well versed in English (B)/that they (C)/had expected (D).
2. He not only comes (A)/here for having lunch (B)/but also for having a glimpse of (C)/the beautiful sales girls (D).
3. I cannot permit you (A)/to leave the class (B)/unless the teacher comes (C)/and instructs me in the matter (D).
4. The patient would not (A)/have died (B)/when the doctor had (C)/come in time (D).
5. Three years have passed (A)/that I returned from (B)/USA and settled here (C).
6. The captain asked (A)/the players to go (B)/to market and buy some fruits (C)/as apples, oranges, bananas etc. (D).
7. Both the rich (A)/along with the poor (B)/are responsible for a great many vices (C)/with which our country is inflicted (D).
8. Since the festival of Diwali is approaching (A)/so my son has bought (B)/many fireworks (C)/as rockets, crackers etc. (D).

9. The thief had (A)/hardly put the cash (B)/in his pocket (C)/then the owner woke up (D).
10. No sooner did we (A)/find out a solution (B)/to the problem (C)/when another problem cropped up (D).

Exercise 18

1. She has lots of money (A)/and she dare not (B)/purchase a new car (C).
2. She is (A)/sympathetic to the rich patients (B)/but also to the poor ones (C).
3. Because she is intelligent (A)/therefore she secures highest marks (B)/in her class (C).
4. It was almost five months ago (A)/since she wrote a letter (B)/to me (C)/to remind me of my promise (D).
5. The inspector was doubtful (A)/that the man who had been run over (B)/by the truck had (C)/lain there for more than a day (D).
6. He instructed me (A)/that I should do (B)/all the work as quickly (C)/like him (D).
7. Seldom or (A)/ever have I sent (B)/a beggar away without (C)/giving him something (D).
8. Seldom or ever (A)/have I tried my (B)/best to help my friends (C)/who are in need (D).
9. The teacher advised (A)/the students to (B)/go through the notes as many times as possible (C)/lest they would fail (D).
10. He asked me (A)/that why I was not appearing (B)/in the examination (C).
11. Most of the founding fathers (A)/of our constitution are (B)/so reverend as Ambedkar (C)/if not more (D).
12. I don't know (A)/if any of the members (B)/of the society is conspiring (C)/against the chairman or not (D).
13. This is the same dog (A)/which bit her (B)/while she was going (C)/to the hospital (D).
14. This is not (A)/such a big problem (B)/which cannot be solved (C)/with some efforts (D).
15. As he is (A)/a perfectionist (B)/so he always insists (C)/on regular practice (D).

ADJECTIVES/DETERMINERS

Exercise 19

1. Kolkata is further (A)/from Alwar (B)/than Jaipur (C)/the capital of Rajasthan (D).
2. Ramesh is smarter (A)/enough to get (B)/selected for this (C)/post, without any recommendations (D).

3. He said, "Priyanka (A)/is the most unique (B)/singer of (C)/our college" (D).
4. This shirt is (A)/comparatively better (B)/than that (C)/we saw in corner shop yesterday (D).
5. Everyone was surprised to note (A)/that Rahim married a girl (B)/ who was more beautiful and more tall (C)/than he (D).
6. A lots of books (A)/on English grammar are (B)/available with me but (C)/this one is the best (D).
7. I told her (A)/that it would be all (B)/the more better (C)/if she herself talked to the groom (D).
8. She does not have (A)/some money to buy (B)/a new refrigerator (C)/so she is worried (D).
9. Now a days (A)/the weather (B)/is getting more cold (C)/and colder (D).
10. All the books (A)/were indeed interesting (B)/but that one was (C)/the more interesting (D).
11. There were only two (A)/warriors but each and every (B)/warrior was equal (C)/ to six persons (D).
12. Whole the chapter (A)/of this grammar book is full of errors (B)/that shows the (C)/carelessness of the proof reader (D).
13. Can we rely (A)/on this agency (B)/for the last news (C)/of the day (D)?
14. Ram is junior than (A)/Shyam and (B)/Ram is older (C)/than Ganesh (D).
15. The militants (A)/entered the palace (B)/from the utmost gate (C)/ with guns hidden in their clothes (D).
16. "She can't sing (A)/much than (B)/four songs at (C)/a stretch", he informed (D).
17. It is well known (A)/that Mrs Indira Gandhi (B)/was the first statesman (C)/of her time (D).

ADVERBS

Exercise 20

1. "Under no circumstances (A)/we can help you (B)/in this immoral project", (C)/ said the Chairman (D).
2. Somebody informed (A)/the contractor that his (B)/brother had only died (C)/ five days before (D).
3. She is very senior(A)/to me, so I (B)/cannot defy her orders (C).
4. Who can believe (A)/that she was not (B)/hardly hit (C)/by the death of her son (D).
5. Hardly she likes (A)/to hear my name (B)/after the dispute which occurred (C)/ between us last year (D).

6. Only by discussing with (A)/the officer concerned (B)/they found out (C)/the person behind the fraud (D).
7. The house is very good (A)/but too much small (B)/to accommodate (C)/the full family (D).
8. He does not (A)/know to make (B)/friends so he is leading (C)/a lonely life (D).
9. Every member of the family (A)/is addicted to drinking (B)/and so Asha is (C).
10. He was very tired (A)/of work so he said (B)/that he would (C)/not accompany us (D)/No error (E).

Exercise 21

1. Sakshi was exorbitantly paid (A)/for how skilful she (B)/welcomed the visitors (C).
2. She is almost quite competent (A)/for the post of Marketing Executive (B)/so if given a chance (C)/she can show the results (D).
3. The student requested (A)/the principal to be enough kind (B)/to grant him seven days leave (C).
4. He has been trying (A)/to persuade her for several months (B)/but he has (C)/not still succeeded (D).
5. Before the game he felt surely (A)/of wining, but within five minutes (B)/he realised that he was wrong (C).
6. The amount which the company (A)/paid to the dependents of (B)/the deceased was (C)/fairly unjustified (D).
7. Although he only earns (A)/sixteen hundred rupees per month (B)/ yet he manages his (C)/family well (D).
8. I liked that opportune moment (A)/where the workers proved themselves (B)/ and came out victorious (C).
9. Where else (A)/did you go besides (B)/the bank (C)?
10. Hàrdly ever (A)/see him (B)/because in my opinion (C)/he is not a reliable man (D)/No error (E).
11. He is a linguist (A)/and always tries to (B)/make his students (C)/ pronounce the words correctly (D).

VERBS

Exercise 22

1. He ordered (A)/as if he (B)/was my master (C).
2. God saves (A)/the queen of Victoria (B).
3. If it was so (A)/poetry (B)/would cease to matter (C).

4. The merit (A)/of these books (B)/are known to everyone (C).
5. The condition of (A)/people living in (B)/rural area (C)/are very bad (D).
6. The smell (A)/of these rose (B)/flowers are (C)/very sweet (D).
7. The condolence messages (A)/received on the (B)/death of Mrs. Gandhi (C)/speaks highly of her greatness (D).
8. Economic cooperation (A)/between the two countries (B)/have increased substantially (C).
9. A band of musicians (A)/have been engaged (B)/for the inauguration function (C).
10. The number (A)/of persons interested (B)/in psychology are (C)/generally small (D).

Exercise 23

1. The manager's comments (A)/on the preparation of the test matches (B)/for this tour (C)/has been generally praised (D).
2. The details (A)/of the incident (B)/was not known (C)/to me (D).
3. The majority of (A)/writers never (B)/passes this stage (C).
4. A large part of (A)/the distinctive features (B)/of the mind is due to its being (C)/an instrument of communication (D).
5. A part of (A)/the mango (B)/are rotten (C)/No error (D).
6. The governing body at (A)/its first meeting (B)/have decided (C)/to conduct the test again (D).
7. The banker's association (A)/has submitted a memorandum (B)/for the fulfilment of (C)/their demands (D).
8. Five quintals of wooden coal (A)/are (B)/his annual requirement (C)/for the unit (D).
9. Dickens have criticised (A)/the philosophy (B)/in 'Hard Times' (C).

Exercise 24

1. All his money (A)/is spent (B)/and all his (C)/hopes ruined (D).
2. This rule may (A)/and ought to be (B)/disregarded for the time being (C).
3. He is one of the (A)/richest man (B)/if not the richest man (C)/in the world (D).
4. We can almost get (A)/everything in (B)/this market (C).
5. Every (A)/Tom, Dick and Harry (B)/drink wine these days (C).
6. He and I (A)/is partners in (B)/this firm (C).
7. He is one of the (A)/great man (B)/that have ever lived (C).

8. The magistrate and collector (A)/were (B)/present there (C)/on the spot (D).
9. Horse and Carriage (A)/are (B)/waiting there (C)/for the couple (D).
10. Rice and fish (A)/are (B)/my favourite dish (C).

Exercise 25

1. He is one of the (A)/tallest man (B)/if not the tallest man (C)/in the city (D).
2. He made a blunder (A)/and worse than (B)/that a crime (C).
3. The wheat (A)/on this farm (B)/is finer than (C)/last year (D).
4. I scarcely have (A)/enough silk (B)/for my saree (C).
5. Every day (A)/and every night (B)/bring its (C)/own pleasures for every one (D).
6. He more than (A)/his parents (B)/are responsible (C)/for his bad habits (D).
7. Bread and butter (A)/are (B)/a rich and nourishing food (C).
8. Not only she (A)/but all her sisters (B)/has been married (C)/since long (D).
9. There are (A)/nothing but (B)/miseries in her life (C).
10. Either he (A)/or I is (B)/responsible for the loss (C).

MISCELLANEOUS

Exercise 26

1. Myself and Ganesh (A)/will take care of (B)/the function (C)/on Sunday (D).
2. The SP has declared that those who are found (A)/guilty of breach of law (B)/or of taking the law into their hands (C)/they will be taken to task (D).
3. In spite of a thoroughly search (A)/of the business premises, the (B)/tax authorities could not find (C)/any incriminating documents (D)/ No error (E). ***(Bank PO)***
4. The last of the Mughal (A)/emperors of India was imprisoned (B)/ and was later sent into (C)/exile by the British (D)/No error (E).
5. Hardly as I stepped (A)/out of my house when (B)/I saw some policemen (C)/ coming towards my house (D)/No error (E). ***(Bank PO)***
6. Swati has such a fine (A)/memory that she can (B)/recollect anything what (C)/ happened many years ago (D)/No error (E).
7. In the meeting, Mr. Mehta's (A)/ suggestions with regard for (B)/certain administrative reforms were (C)/hailed by all the members (D)/No error (E). ***(Bank PO)***
8. Children who have had (A)/good pre-school education (B)/are most likely to out-do (C)/other children at school (D)/No error (E).
9. If I knew (A)/that my friend had planned (B)/to visit the town today (C)/, I would have made his stay comfortable (D). ***(SCRA)***
10. When the dentist came in (A)/my tooth was stopped aching (B)/out of fear (C)/ that I might lose my tooth (D).

Exercise 27

1. From Bombay (A)/the Rajdhani Express (B)/do not go straight (C)/to New Delhi (D)/No error (E). ***(BSRB)***

2. It couldn't have been (A)/written by Kalidas because (B)/that kind of dress was not worn (C)/till after his death (D)/No error (E).

3. Harish is (A)/very much (B)/willing to (C)/come with you (D)/No error (E). ***(BSRB)***

4. The lady said that (A)/she should be away (B)/from home tomorrow as Malati's (C)/friend had come to visit Mumbai (D)/No error (E).

5. Journey by car is (A)/as quick or perhaps quicker (B)/than by train (C)/in this particular case (D)/No error (E). ***(BSRB)***

6. He asked what the weather (A)/had been like (B)/during my holidays and I said (C)/that it had been awful (D)/No error (E).

7. You are lucky (A)/to get (B)/such a (C)/well paid job (D)/No error (E). ***(BSRB)***

8. If I would have (A)/spoken to my father (B)/as you speak to me (C)/he would have beaten me (D)/No error (E). ***(BSRB)***

9. We are quite fond (A)/of this house (B)/because we are living in it (C)/for the last five years (D)/No error (E).

10. Not for nothing (A)/did he prosper (B)/as a business consultant (C)/since his arrival in America 20 years ago (D)/No error (E).

Exercise 28

1. This type of product (A)/is not available in (B)/any of the shop (C)/ in the market around plaza (D)/No error (E). ***(Bank PO)***

2. Hardly had I (A)/reached the airport where (B)/I learn about (C)/the powerful bomb explosion (D)/No error (E).

3. As a practice (A)/the last batch of (B)/the tins undergoes (C)/through check up (D)/No error (E). ***(Bank PO)***

4. One of my brother (A)/told me about (B)/the sad demise (C)/of your uncle (D)/ No error (E).

5. He is not only (A)/sincere towards his responsibilities (B)/but also very competent (C)/to handle the job (D)/No error (E). ***(Bank PO)***

6. The minister along with his (A)/party colleagues have (B)/been given a warm (C)/reception at the function (D)/No error (E). ***(Bank PO)***

7. You should not be (A)/so quick in giving (B)/advice lest you will be (C)/perceived as interfering in others affairs (D)/No error (E). ***(Bank PO)***

8. Because of his (A)/innocence he cannot (B)/distinguish a cheat (C)/ for an honest person (D)/No error (E).

9. Every day when he (A)/passes through this side (B)/all the employee gather (C)/ around to have a glimpse. (D)/No error (E). ***(Bank PO)***

10. He said that (A)/if I found the front door locked (B)/I was to go round (C)/to the back (D)/No error (E). ***(BSRB)***

Exercise 29

1. These acts were (A)/pushed through Parliament (B)/in spite of opposition (C)/ but for little modification (D)/No error (E). ***(State Bank PO)***

2. The man who is (A)/perpetually hesitating (B)/which of the two things (C)/do first will ultimately do either (D)/No error (E). ***(State Bank PO)***

3. No hill station (A)/is as beautiful (B)/as Darjeeling (C)/with its scenic beauty (D)/No error (E). ***(State Bank PO)***

4. On my request (A)/Jatin introduced me (B)/to his friend (C)/who is singer and scientist (D)/No error (E). ***(State Bank PO)***

5. One of the most (A)/widely spread (B)/bad habit (C)/is the use of tobacco (D)/No error (E).

6. Being a well known (A)/cartoonist, he was (B)/invited to deliver (C)/a lecture on Modern art (D)/No error (E). ***(State Bank PO)***

7. The chief idea of every common type of traveller (A)/is to see(B)/as many objects (C)/of interest as possibly he could (D)/No error (E). ***(State Bank PO)***

8. Atul's habit of (A)/delaying his work (B)/puts his colleagues (C)/to a lot of trouble (D)/No error (E). ***(State Bank PO)***

9. My brother has been (A)/living in America (B)/with his family (C)/for the past ten years (D)/No error (E). ***(State Bank PO)***

10. I did not like (A)/going to night school (B)/but I had no alternative (C)/as I have to work in day time (D)/No error (E). ***(BSRB)***

Exercise 30

1. All the people living (A)/in the house (B)/including the servant (C)/was invited there (D)/No error (E). ***(BSRB)***

2. Mahesh thought that he (A)/would pass the examination (B)/ although he did not answer (C)/most of the questions correct (D)/ No error (E). ***(BSRB)***

3. The robbers were (A)/caught just as they (B)/were about to (C)/escape from the jail (D)/No error (E).

4. Nobody believed him (A)/when he said that (B)/his son was gone (C)/out of the country (D)/No error (E).

5. As soon as he (A)/opened the old (B)/wooden box than a rat (C)/jumped out of it (D)/No error (E).

6. Hardly did she went (A)/out of her house (B)/when the postman came (C)/with the telegram (D)/No error (E).

7. The faster he completes (A)/the work given to (B)/him, the largest (C)/will be his profit (D)/No error (E).

8. There has not been (A)/any rain fall in this (B)/part of the country (C)/since the last two years (D)/No error (E). ***(BSRB)***

9. He has not only built (A)/this big theatre but also (B)/ a few (C)/bungalows in this city (D)/No error (E).

10. Kunal's father advised (A)/him not to (B)/ride the motorcycle (C)/lately at night (D)/No error (E). ***(BSRB)***

Exercise 31

1. He says that (A)/he has (B)/a car (C)/beside a scooter (D).

2. If I was you (A)/I would not have (B)/committed (C)/this blunder (D).

3. Not one of the hundreds (A)/of striking workers (B)/were allowed to go (C)/near the factory (D).

4. Did you see (A)/any of the child (B)/when you were (C)/in the garden ? (D)/No error (E). ***(BSRB)***

5. The boy asked (A)/his father why (B)/he cutting (C)/down the tree (D)/No error (E).

6. The applicant (A)/being a house holder (B)/he is (C)/entitled to vote (D)/No error (E).

7. He walked (A)/quick so that (B)/he would not (C)/be late (D)/No error (E). ***(BSRB)***

8. The teacher said (A)/that Ajay was (B)/capable of doing (C)/more better work (D)/No error (E). ***(BSRB)***

9. Dinesh exercise (A)/every day so (B)/that he may (C)/keep himself healthy (D)/ No error (E).

10. The thirsty (A)/children drank (B)/up all (C)/the water (D)/No error (E).

Exercise 32

1. One of his many (A)/good traits that (B)/come to my mind (C)/was his modesty (D)/No error (E). ***(BSRB)***

2. He has a scheme (A)/of his own which (B)/he thinks preferable (C)/than that of any other person (D)/No error (E). ***(BSRB)***

3. Ten new members (A)/have been enrolled (B)/and seven have (C)/resigned (D)/ No error (E). ***(BSRB)***

4. Children visiting the (A)/park are amused (B)/by the monkeys (C)/play in their cages (D). ***(SBI PO)***

5. The man told to her (A)/that he had not brought his dog (B)/out for a walk (C)/as he was afraid that it would rain (D).

6. I am sure that (A)/neither the house (B)/nor its contents (C)/is for sale (D). *(Asstt. Grade)*

7. The Hindi and the Marathi are (A)/different forms of Sanskrit language (B)/ which was once spoken (C)/in almost every part of India (D). *(Bank PO)*

8. The Committee Chief warned the party members (A)/that if they persist (B)/in their obstructionist attitude (C)/they would be suspended (D). *(CDS)*

9. The agitating students had taken (A)/a vow not to return to their (B)/classes until their demands were not (C)/accepted by the Principal (D)/No error (E). *(Bank PO)*

10. Today, the cost of living (A)/is such higher that many (B)/people find it difficult to (C)/keep their hearts burning (D)/No error (E). *(Bank PO)*

Exercise 33

1. When Charles was (A)/in the hospital (B)/his sister sent (C)/much fruit than his uncle (D)/No error (E).

2. Mr. Sharma has (A)/driven almost twice (B)/so far as (C)/Mr. Khanna has (D)/ No error (E). *(Regional Rural)*

3. All the players (A)/except Samuel (B)/were present (C)/on the field (D)/No error (E). *(Regional Rural Bank)*

4. The teacher drew (A)/an attention of the (B)/boys to the importance (C)/of regular practice (D)/No error (E).

5. The doctor advised (A)/Suresh and Ramesh for going swimming (B)/because it was (C)/good for them (D)/No error (E). *(Regional Rural Bank)*

6. I am not (A)/wealthy so I (B)/cannot afford to buy (C)/a expensive car (D)/No error (E). *(Regional Rural Bank)*

7. Kamala worked very (A)/hard so that she (B)/might not keep the others (C)/wait too long (D)/No error (E).

8. The teacher was (A)/busy and asked (B)/three of we to divide the (C)/work and do it (D)/No error (E). *(Regional Rural Bank)*

9. The ruling party stood (A)/for implementation of the Bill (B)/and was ready to stake (C)/their political existence (D).

10. The interviewer asked (A)/the candidate (B)/to what district (C)/he came from (D). *(SSC)*

Exercise 34

1. Two people the (A)/clerk and the (B)/typist helps me (C)/in my office (D)/No error (E). *(Regional Rural Bank)*

2. The short boy (A)/has seven rupees (B)/and the fat boy (C)/has only a rupee (D)/ No error (E). *(Regional Rural Bank)*

3. Inspite of the doctor's (A)/stern warning (B)/he continued taking (C)/sugar in his tea (D). ***(Stenographer's Exam)***

4. Never set a bad (A)/example; always remember that (B)/good and bad behaviour is inculcated by example (C).

5. For young Minu (A)/peace in Kashmir (B)/is almost terrible (C)/as war (D).

6. Being a very hot day (A)/all of us remained at home (B)/and watched television and (C)/enjoyed ourselves the whole day (D).

7. Had the function (A)/not been postponed (B)/because of the strike (C)/she may have been able to participate (D).

8. The teacher was (A)/very busy and so asked three (B)/of we to divide (C)/the work and complete it (D).

9. Neelima has such a fine (A)/memory that she can (B)/recollect any thing (C)/what happened even many years ago (D).

10. In a fit of temper (A)/he tore up a sweet letter (B)/which his wife had (C)/written to him (D)/No error (E). ***(BSRB)***

Exercise 35

1. Every leaf (A)/and every flower proclaim (B)/the glory of God (C)/No error (D). ***(Income Tax)***

2. My house (A)/is better (B)/than John (C)/No error (D). ***(Hotel Management)***

3. To perform (A)/this experiment (B)/drop little sugar (C)/into a glass of water (D).

4. As he had taken (A)/only a few sips (B)/there was still little water (C)/left in the glass (D).

5. For her sake as well as for John (A)/I hoped fervently (B)/that she might still be found (C)/No error (D). ***(MBA)***

6. Is there any other reasons (A)/that you can give us for your failure (B)/to take action as you promised (C)/No error (D). ***(MBA)***

7. The future is (A)/yet to come (B)/but you have (C)/right to shape it (D). ***(BSRB)***

8. He won't (A)/return the money (B)/that he borrowed (C)/won't he? (D).

9. Money not only satisfies (A)/the basic psychological needs (B)/but also the (C)/higher order psychological needs (D)/No error (E). ***(BSRB)***

10. All I know is that (A)/I won't be at peace (B)/with my self (C)/unless I do not go there (D)/No error (E). ***(BSRB)***

Exercise 36

1. A nationwide survey (A)/has brought up an (B)/interesting finding (C)/regarding infant mortality rate in India (D).
2. Troy was taken (A)/by Greeks; (B)/this formed the basis of the story (C)/which has become famous (D).
3. Whatever his intention may be (A)/he should consider them carefully (B)/before he comes to a decision (C)/No error (D). *(MBA)*
4. These kind of shoes (A)/seem to be expensive (B)/but they are relatively easy to care for (C)/No error (D).
5. The reason we have not been (A)/able to pay income tax (B)/is due to the fact (C)/that we did not receive pay on time (D).
6. A person I met (A)/in the theatre (B)/was the playwright (C)/himself (D).
7. Dr. Chandra (A)/is only dentist (B)/in (C)/our village (D).
8. The majority of the (A)/computer professionals recommends (B)/that effective measures (C)/should be taken against software piracy (D).
9. The accelerating pace of life (A)/in our city (B)/has had a tremendous effect (C)/on the culture and life-style of the people (D)/No error (E).
10. You are never practical (A)/and your suggestions (B)/hold no water (C)/because they are not convincing (D).

Exercise 37

1. I am (A)/better acquainted (B)/with this area (C)/than you (D)/No error (E). *(SBI PO)*
2. It is said (A)/by some persons (B)/that one of the nationalised bank (C)/has started a new scheme of lending (D)/No error (E).
3. The boy who (A)/you see there (B)/made the top score (C)/in the last match (D)/No error (E).
4. Being occupied (A)/with some important matters, (B)/he had no time (C)/to attend the meetings (D)/No error (E).
5. The sun whose (A)/ray give life to the (B)/earth was venerated as (C)/God by our ancestors (D)/No error (E).
6. He was not promoted (A)/to the rank of colonel (B)/till for a few (C)/months of his retirement. (D)/No error (E). *(SBI PO)*
7. Our soldiers (A)/were better trained (B)/than that (C)/of enemies (D)/No error (E).
8. If it were possible (A)/to get near when (B)/one of the volcanic eruptions take place (C)/we could see a grand sight (D)/No error (E).
9. Had I come(A)/to know about(B)/his difficulties(C)/I would have certainly helped him (D)/No error (E).
10. Being a very (A)/hot day (B)/I (C)/remained indoors (D).

Exercise 38

1. The demand of the citizen's (A)/forum that the prices of essential (B)/commodities to lower down will (C)/soon be considered by the Government (D)/No error (E). ***(Regional Rural Bank)***
2. Despite of a good monsoon (A)/this year, the production (B)/of foodgrains in the (C)/country did not go up (D)/No error (E). ***(Bank PO)***
3. Whatever work (A)/that which you undertake (B)/put your best efforts (C)/to achieve success (D).
4. As it was Ranjan's (A)/first interview he dressed himself (B)/in his most (C)/ formal suit (D). ***(Bank PO)***
5. The party chief made it a point to state that (A)/the Prime Minister and the Union Home Minister (B)/should also come (C)/and see what his party men had seen (D).
6. It is not difficult to believe that a man (A)/who has lived in this city (B)/for a long time (C)/he will never feel at home anywhere else in the world (D). ***(NBA)***
7. If the teacher is good (A)/the students (B)/will respond (C)/positively to them (D). ***(BSRB)***
8. Mr. Sharma, our representative, (A)/will (B)/attend the meeting (C)/on our behalf (D)/No error (E).
9. One must use (A)/his best efforts (B)/if one (C)/wishes to succeed (D)/No error (E).
10. It is suggested that (A)/a ring road (B)/should be built (C)/to relieve the congestion (D)/No error (E). ***(SBI PO)***

Exercise 39

1. Even though he found the subject (A)/rather interesting Raghu could not (B)/ manage good marks (C)/in the examination (D)/No error (E). ***(BSRB Clerk)***
2. The enemity between the (A)/two groups had reached a level (B)/where reconciliations has (C)/become impossible (D)/No error (E). ***(BSRB Clerk)***
3. My father was (A)/in (B)/bad mood (C)/yesterday morning (D).
4. Sunita opened a almirah (A)/full of books (B)/and took one book (C)/for reading (D).
5. According to the Bible (A)/it is meek and humble (B)/who shall (C)/inherit the earth (D).
6. Now that she is living in her own flat, (A)/she cleans the windows, (B)/twice a week in the summer (C)/and once a week in the winter (D)/No error (E).
7. After looking through many (A)/advertisements Sudhir decide (B)/ to buy the cheapest (C)/brand in the market (D)/No error (E). ***(BSRB Clerk)***

8. The interviewer asked me (A)/if I knew that (B)/Kalidas was the greater (C)/than any other poet (D)/No error (E). ***(BSRB Clerk)***

9. Mr. Smith was accused for murder (A)/but the court found him (B)/not guilty (C)/and acquitted him (D).

10. It is not possible (A)/for me (B)/to exchange the goods (C)/once the sale has been completed (D)/No error (E). ***(Stenographer's Exam)***

Exercise 40

1. This town isn't very (A)/well known (B)/and there isn't much to see (C)/so a few tourists come here (D).

2. On my request (A)/Sarita introduced me (B)/to her friend (C)/who is singer and a scientist (D).

3. Aruna was (A)/unhappy about the results (B)/of the discussion she (C)/has with Rashmi (D)/No error (E). ***(BSRB Clerk)***

4. He was driving slowly (A)/down the highway (B)/when a cat ran (C)/across and he had to brake all of a sudden (D)/No error (E). ***(BSRB Clerk)***

5. It being rainy day (A)/most of the people (B)/out on the street were (C)/carrying umbrellas (D)/No error (E). ***(BSRB Clerk)***

6. The need to set up (A)/a good library in the locality (B)/has been in the minds of people (C)/for some time (D)/No error (E). ***(BSRB Clerk)***

7. The road (A)/to famous monument (B)/passes through (C)/a forest (D).

8. Several prominent figures (A)/involved in the scandal (B)/are required to appear (C)/to the investigation committee (D).

9. To make him succeed (A)/the correct thing to do (B)/is to punish him (C)/until he does not try (D)/No error (E). ***(BSRB Clerk)***

10. C.V. Raman was one of those great sons of India (A)/who has earned everlasting fame (B)/for scientific researches (C)/No error (D). ***(NDA 1993)***

Exercise 41

1. Whenever they passes (A)/through this city (B)/they never forget to (C)/come to our house (D)/No error (E). ***(BSRB)***

2. Children often (A)/quarrel on (B)/petty (C)/issues (D).

3. When the teachers are on strike (A)/and a notice to this effect (B)/is pasted on the college gate (C)/there is no sense to go there (D).

4. Young children should not sit close (A)/to the TV set (B)/as it affects (C)/on their eyes (D).

5. I am vexed (A)/at him (B)/about what (C)/he has done (D).

6. The girls were playing (A)/outside the house whereas (B)/the boys were sitting (C)/inside and played cards (D)/No error (E).

7. The policemen started (A)/firing the crowd (B)/when the striking (C)/student turned violent (D)/No error (E). ***(BSRB)***

8. He was about to telling (A)/the investigators the truth (B)/when his companion (C)/suddenly interrupted him (D)/No error (E).

9. Mohini washes all her (A)/clothes and cooks food (B)/for the family before (C)/ she going to the office (D)/No error (E).

10. Praveen is so good (A)/a batsman that (B)/he would be certainly (C)/included in the team (D)/No error (E). ***(BSRB)***

Exercise 42

1. Our Mathematics teacher (A)/often emphasises on (B)/the need for (C)/a lot of practice (D).

2. We could not see (A)/the places clear (B)/as the train was (C)/moving very fast (D)/No error (E).

3. Although the patient (A)/was rudely with the (B)/ nurses he behaved (C)/nicely with the doctor (D)/No error (E).

4. Although the driver applied (A)/the brakes he could (B)/not prevent the bus (C)/ from hit the tree (D)/No error (E). ***(BSRB)***

5. Dileep's performance in the (A)/film was worst than (B)/Amit's but was not (C)/as bad as Vipul's (D)/No error (E). ***(BSRB)***

6. This kind of behaviour (A)/has not been (B)/seen here (C)/since the last four years (D).

7. Rekha was trying for admission (A)/in the Engineering College (B)/ even though her parents wanted (C)/her to take up medicine (D).

8. As the party was going (A)/we noticed Mr. Roy fall back (B)/in his chair (C)/ gasping for breath (D). ***(Assistant Grade)***

9. Of all the men (A)/known to me none is (B)/inclined (C)/to think ill to others (D).

10. In a report issued by Indian Statistical Institute (A)/the Iron and Steel industry (B)/is investing more than any other (C)/Indian Industry, in fighting pollution (D)/No error (E). ***(Central Excise)***

Exercise 43

1. Monisha was the about (A)/tell her teacher the (B)/truth when her (C)/friend interrupted her (D)/No error (E). ***(BSRB Clerk)***

2. Prayag and Parag used (A)/to work for almost twelve (B)/hours in the factory (C)/they are working earlier (D)/No error (E).

3. After toiling very hard (A)/over a long period of time, (B)/he found that people recognised him (C)/as a successful person (D)/No error (E).

4. The angry man walked hurriedly (A)/into the crowded room (B)/and shouted loud (C)/at the guests (D).

5. He ran so fastly (A)/that he reached (B)/the destination in (C)/just two minutes (D)/No error (E). ***(BSRB Clerk)***

6. Although he is usually (A)/rude with everyone (B)/he behaved nice with (C)/all of us today (D)/No error (E).

7. Anjali's performance in the (A)/drama was best than (B)/Deepali's but not (C)/as good as Vaishali's (D)/No error (E).

8. The firemen could not (A)/succeed in rescue the (B)/child although they (C)/ could put out the fire (D)/No error (E).

9. Whenever they go out (A)/for swimming they (B)/take their (C)/ blue bag with them (D)/No error (E).

10. He was fascinated by insects (A)/and the more he studied (B)/their habits (C)/ greater was his fascination (D). ***(Railways Rec. Board)***

Exercise 44

1. Everyone felt that (A)/the big glittering (B)/diamond (C)/was most unique (D).

2. I advised my son (A)/to engage two coolies instead of one (B)/because the luggage was too much (C)/heavy for a single coolie (D).

3. The children were (A)/playing with a ball (B)/and run around when (C)/the accident occurred (D)/No error (E).

4. Avinash is not so (A)/good a batsman to be(B)/selected for the (C)/national cricket team (D)/No error (E). ***(BSRB Clerk)***

5. I tried on (A)/both the dresses (B)/and finally decided (C)/to buy the least expensive one (D).

6. He ultimately decided (A)/to willingly and cheerfully accept(B)/the responsibility (C)/entrusted to him (D).

7. Being the only (A)/people present there (B)/their presence was (C)/most important (D).

8. Firstly you should (A)/think over the meaning (B)/of the words (C)/and then use them (D).

9. By all standards (A)/he is a best soldier (B)/our military school (C)/ has produced so far (D).

10. My friends insisted (A)/that I should (B)/see the movie (C)/from beginning to the end (D). ***(UDC)***

Exercise 45

1. The car flew off the road (A)/and fell into the valley (B)/because Anish (C)/was driving faster (D). ***(SBI PO)***
2. Watch how careful (A)/the sparrow knits the (B)/straws into one another (C)/to form a nest ? (D). ***(Bank PO)***
3. Of all the friends (A)/I have had (B)/he is the most helpful (C)/and less arrogant (D).
4. The audience (A)/are requested to be (B)/in its seats (C)/No error (D). ***(SSC Exam)***
5. The reason we have not been able to pay income tax (A)/is due to the fact (B)/that we did not receive pay on time (C). ***(SSC Exam)***
6. The Prime Minister has said that India would not have spent so much on defence (A)/if some of the neighbouring countries (B)/adopted the policy of restricting defence expenditure (C)/No error (D).
7. With little patience (A)/you will (B)/be able to (C)/cross this hurdle (D).
8. My brother in laws (A)/who live in Bombay (B)/have come to stay with us (D)/No error (E).
9. Sheila Chandra began her concert by chanting Om (A)/turning it finally into an experience (B)/close with prayer (C)/No error (D). ***(NDA 1993)***
10. I advised my son (A)/to engage two coolies instead of one (B)/ because the luggage was too much heavy for a single coolie (C)/ No error (D). ***(NDA)***

Exercise 46

1. As there was only one taxi available (A)/I had no other alternative (B)/but to pay the fare demanded by the driver (C)/No error (D). ***(SSC Exam)***
2. Good night (A)/I am glad (B)/to see you (C)/No error (D).
3. We all (A)/take vegetable (B)/and fruit (C)/No error (D).
4. Geometry and Drawing (A)/are more easier (B)/than (C)/Geography and Social Studies (D). ***(NDA)***
5. He is (A)/too intelligent (B)/to make (C)/a mistake (D)/No error (E).
6. My observation (A)/is that (B)/between Vivek and Shashi (C)/Vivek is the most intelligent (D). ***(Bank PO)***
7. She saw that there was nothing else (A)/she could do (B)/because the room was as clean as (C)/it has never been before (D).
8. It is the duty of every citizen (A)/to do his utmost (B)/to defend the hardly won (C)/freedom of the country (D).
9. Even though it was (A)/raining heavy (B)/I went out (C)/to get some medicines (D). ***(Bank PO)***
10. Inspite of working (A)/very neat and careful (B)/he could not win (C)/even the third prize (D).

Exercise 47

1. On his attitude (A)/it seems that he wants (B)/is that the decision making power (C)/should rest with him (D). ***(Bank PO)***
2. A large scale exchange of nuclear weapons (A)/will produce unprecedented amounts of radiation (B)/that can penetrate into the environment (C). ***(Assistant Grade)***
3. I have advised my brother (A)/to dispose of (B)/his old car and (C)/buy new one (D).
4. My uncle frequently (A)/goes to abroad (B)/on business (C)/by air (D). ***(NDA)***
5. Our laxity in duty (A)/increases (B)/with our (C)/aversion for work (D). ***(I. Tax)***
6. It is wrong (A)/on your part to call into (B)/question the integrity (C)/of your younger brother (D).
7. Globalization is not likely (A)/to usher (B)/economic progress of (C)/the country as we are expecting (D).
8. The situation is so tense (A)/in the city that (B)/even a small incident can spark (C)/communal riots in the city (D).
9. The world (A)/comprises (B)/good and bad people (C)/ No error (D).
10. Two thirds of the book (A)/were (B)/rubbish (C)/No error (D). ***(CDS 1993)***

Exercise 48

1. He will certainly help (A)/if you will ask him (B)/in a pleasant manner (C)/No error (D). ***(CDS)***
2. The warden (A)/forbade the student (B)/from leaving the hostel (C)/No error (D).
3. You must either tell me (A)/the whole story or at least (B)/the first half of it (C)/ No error (D).
4. Twice twelve (A)/makes (B)/twenty four (C)/No error (D). ***(CDS)***
5. It is necessary (A)/that everybody (B)/must have a house (C)/No error (D). ***(CDS)***
6. The school is (A)/within hundred yards (B)/from the church (C)/No error (D).
7. It is easy to see that (A)/a lawyer's demeanour in court (B)/may be prejudicial against the interests of his client (C)/No error (D). ***(CDS)***
8. I am hearing (A)/a lot about (B)/the problem of AIDS these days (C)/No error (D).
9. You can get (A)/all the informations you want (B)/in this book (C)/ No error (D). ***(CDS)***
10. He persisted (A)/to do it (B)/in spite of my sincere advice (C)/No error (D). ***(CDS)***

Exercise 49

1. That house (A)/is costing me (B)/ten lac rupees (C)/No error (D). **(CDS)**

2. I wonder (A)/how am I (B)/to do it (C)/No error (D). **(CDS)**

3. A recent study has (A)/indicated that there (B)/is perceptible change in (C)/the attitudes of the people (D).

4. If a man diligently seeks to come into contact (A)/with the best that has been thought (B)/and said in this world (C)/he will become simple and selfish (D)/No error (E).

5. I go to (A)/the bed (B)/at eight (C)/every night (D).

6. What will happen (A)/suppose if we (B)/don't meet him (C)/in the banquet hall (D).

7. When asked (A)/about his children (B)/the veteran sportsman said (C)/that his youngest son's health was too good (D).

8. Regardless of (A)/what people (B)/say, I must repeat that these are the facts concerning (C)/the requirements for the position (D)/ No error (E).

9. There is (A)/no objection to us (B)/joining the feast if he is willing (C)/to share the expenses (D).

10. It is duty (A)/to put off our shoes (B)/before entering the sanctum sanctorum of any temple or mosque (C)/No error (D). **(NDA)**

Exercise 50

1. Vishnu was trying to pass (A)/through the gap on (B)/the fence when he (C)/tore his shirt (D)/No error (E).

2. Foolishly Madhu threw (A)/some water on the electric heater (B)/ when it catches fire (C)/and she got a shock (D)/No error (E). **(Bank PO)**

3. Rajesh was expecting (A)/a telegram from his uncle (B)/which would inform (C)/ him whether he should go or not (D)/ No error (E). **(Bank PO)**

4. Neither of the plans (A)/suits him, therefore (B)/he decided not to (C)/go out yesterday (D)/No error (E).

5. In spite of the rumours (A)/of an impending takeover (B)/by government (C)/ Ram Lal bought more shares of that company (D)/ No error (E). **(Bank PO)**

6. Simplest solution (A)/than this expensive (B)/method that you are suggesting (C)/should be found out (D)/No error (E).

7. The book was so (A)/advanced that even (B)/the graduates in the discipline (C)/ found it difficult (D)/No error (E). **(Bank PO)**

8. The only good thing (A)/about these pens (B)/are their colour (C)/No error (D). *(NDA)*

9. She's always (A)/lamenting the lack of sports facilities (B)/in town (C)/No error (D).

10. As we've not (A)/got the proper materials (B)/we'll have just to improvise (C)/No error (D). *(NDA 2005-1)*

Exercise 51

1. He could not plan his strategy(A)/until he knew(B)/whom(C)/his opponents could be (D). *(Railways)*

2. If I were (A)/he, I would have taught (B)/those cheats (C)/a lesson just now (D).

3. Last summer (A)/he went (B)/to his uncle's village, (C)/and enjoyed very much (D). *(CDS)*

4. As I kept a strict watch (A)/with my way of living (B)/I could see that (C)/it was necessary to economize (D)/No error (E). *(BSRB PO)*

5. His father left him a fortune (A)/but he is so extravagant (B)/that he will spent (C)/it all before he is 30 (D)/No error (E).

6. The father told his son (A)/that he was a lazy boy (B)/and that he had done (C)/his work very bad (D)/No error (E). *(BSRB PO)*

7. If I would have realised (A)/what a bad driver you were (B)/I would not have (C)/come with you (D)/No error (E). *(BSRB PO)*

8. He confidently asked the crowd (A)/if they thought that (B)/he was right (C)/and the crowd shouted that they do (D)/No error (E).

9. I saw the accident (A)/but fortunately, I did not have to (B)/give evidence as there were (C)/a large number of other evidences (D)/ No error (E).

10. Arun is not only eminent (A)/for his writings in English (B)/but also for his (C)/paintings on spiritual themes (D)/No error (E). *(BSRB PO)*

Exercise 52

1. I can hear (A)/the bell ringing (B)/but nobody seems to be coming (C)/to opening the door (D)/No error (E). *(BSRB PO)*

2. I have been teaching in this school (A)/since several years (B)/but have never met (C)/such a hopeless class as this (D)/No error (E).

3. When he went out (A)/he left the radio on (B)/so that his parents shall think (C)/that he was still in the house (D)/No error (E). *(BSRB PO)*

4. May I (A)/know who (B)/you want (C)/to see please (D). *(Hotel Management)*

5. Being a destitute, (A)/I admitted him (B)/to an old (C)/people's home (D).

6. There is (A)/no question (B)/of my failing (C)/in the examination (D)/No error (E).

7. The scientist must follow (A)/his hunches and (B)/his data (C)/ wherever it may lead (D). *(Astt. Grade)*

8. Due to me (A)/being a newcomer (B)/I was unable to get a house (C)/suitable for my family (D).

9. I suppose (A)/that you have heard (B)/the latest news (C)/Jack has married that girl (D)/No error (E).

10. Wherever they go (A)/Indians easily (B)/adapt to (C)/the local circumstances (D).

Exercise 53

1. There are a number of reasons (A)/I do not like him, (B)/but his selfishness is intolerable (C)/No error (D). *(CDS 2000)*

2. I have read an interesting book yesterday (A)/and underlined the new words (B)/ which were simple but effective (C)/No error (D).

3. He cannot be trusted (A)/with important secret informations (B)/ otherwise I would have made him my assistant (C)/No error (D). *(CDS 2000)*

4. Is there further reasons (A)/you can give me for your failure (B)/as you promised (C)/No error (D). *(CDS 2000)*

5. During the final minutes of his speech (A)/the speaker requested to (B)/the audience to have patience (C)/No error (D).

6. He is running temperature since last Friday (A)/and doctors suspect (B)/that he is down with typhoid (C)/No error (D).

7. Travel agents around the world have to rely on computers (A)/to book seats in air flights or rooms in hotels, (B)/either now or a year from now (C)/No error (D).

8. She expressed her gratitudes (A)/to all those (B)/who had supported her in election. (C)/No error (D). *(CDS 2000)*

9. When the meeting was over, (A)/he was very tired (B)/so that he went home immediately (C)/No error (D).

10. Modern man must pull himself off together (A)/and act his part in life (B)/as God's own most favourite creature (C)/No error (D). *(CDS 2000)*

Exercise 54

1. The teacher was happy (A)/when he entered the class (B)/which comprised of a hundred students (C)/No error (D).

2 In China, scholars have discovered in a language (A)/that women involved among themselves (B)/with a script that was less complex than the official (C)/No error (D). *(CDS 2001)*

3. In most of the states (A)/forty percent of people under thirty (B)/is undernourished (C)/No error (D).

4. Yet, firms and other concerns are spending large sums of money all time (A)/and somehow we take this for granted (B)/and never stop to wonder where it comes from (C)/No error (D).

5. Scarcely we had finished observing this (A)/when we were surprised by about a dozen of the old birds (B)/jumping in the most unsafe and funny manner towards the sea (C)/No error (D). ***(CDS 2001)***

6. I asked (A)/if she has looked everywhere (B)/and she said 'yes' (C)/No error (D). ***(CDS 2001)***

7. Had I realised (A)/that it was such a long way (B)/I would take a taxi (C)/No error (D).

8. Thank you for your invitation for lunch (A)/which I am very pleased (B)/to accept (C)/No error (D). ***(CDS 2001)***

9. As people keep more animals as pets (A)/more and more animal related law suits (B)/reaching the courts (C)/No error (D).

10. The Brahmins, in the period of their decline, took stock of the situation (A)/and realised where the deficiencies of the ancient creed lied (B)/and how they should be met (C)/No error (D).

Exercise 55

1. Don't think you can say unpleasant things (A)/about someone behind his back (B)/and not found out (C)/No error (D). ***(CDS 2001-II)***

2. The Americans speak (A)/different from us (B)/though our grammar is the same (C)/No error (D).

3. This is an instance (A)/of the blind (B)/leading the blind people (C)/No error (D).

4. He took to drink (A)/to lessen (B)/his mental tension (C)/No error (D). ***(CDS 2001-II)***

5. My father could lead (A)/full and happy life (B)/without spending lot of money (C)/No error (D). ***(CDS 2001-II)***

6. All India Radio broadcasted (A)/a very good programme (B)/this morning (C)/ No error (D).

7. There were so much cattle (A)/on the road that (B)/it was difficult to drive safely (C)/No error (D). ***(CDS 2001-II)***

8. What could have provoked him to behave (A)/in such a manner (B)/at dinner last night ? (C)/No error (D). ***(CDS 2001-II)***

9. They were rich zamindars in the thirties (A)/but now they have fallen on the evil days (B)/and have lost much of their property (C)/ No error (D).

10. The foreign ambassador was (A)/noted for both his charming manners (B)/as well as his wide knowledge of language (C)/No error (D).

Exercise 56

1. Oil has and (A)/still is (B)/in great demand (C)/No error (D). *(CDS 2002)*
2. He worked hard (A)/so he might top the list (B)/and win a medal (C)/No error (D). *(CDS 2002)*
3. Thanks to the efforts of the last batsman (A)/in the moment of crisis (B)/the defeat was averted (C)/No error (D).
4. Dread of hydrogen bomb promotes fanaticism (A)/and fanaticism is more likely than anything else, will lead to (B)/actual use of the hydrogen bomb (C)/No error (D). *(CDS 2002)*
5. Because of the high prices (A)/first they discontinued jam on toasts (B)/and then substituted margarine for butter (C)/ No error (D).
6. The little show was organised (A)/not only for him (B)/but for you and I as well (C)/No error (D).
7. They seem to enjoy (A)/being rung up (B)/in all hours of the day and night (C)/ No error (D). *(CDS 2002)*
8. The right to make war, like the right to strike (A)/but in a far high degree (B)/is very dangerous in a world governed be scientific technique (C)/No error (D).
9. I admit that some newspapers in their bid (A)/to sell more have jettisoned the high standard (B)/that the press in India has followed since years (C)/No error (D). *(CDS 2002)*
10. As the crow put the frog aside in order to sharpen its beak (A)/the frog leapt in the well (B)/and began to croak in derision (C)/No error (D).

Exercise 57

1. We had to cancel our trip to Delhi (A)/because when we reached the railway station (B)/the train left (C)/No error (D).
2. Many a student (A)/has failed in the Mathematics (B)/but Dilip has scored 100 percent (C)/No error (D).
3. The General with over 1000 officers and soldiers (A)/have surrendered to the Indian troops (B)/who are patrolling the valley (C)/No error (D). *(CDS 2002-II)*
4. If he had wrote the examination faster (A)/and answered one more question (B)/ he would have scored better (C)/No error (D).
5. For decades (A)/there have been (B)/a debate on whether schizophrenia is a psychological condition (C)/No error (D).
6. Mohan is the one (A)/who always finds fault (B)/with whatever Ram does (C)/ No error (D). *(CDS 2002-II)*
7. There is a need (A)/to revising government policies (B)/on controlling unauthorised constructions (C)/No error (D).

8. We know where it begins (A)/but we don't know (B)/that where it ends (C)/No error (D). *(CDS 2002-II)*
9. The simplest method (A)/of welding two pieces of metal together (B)/is known as pressure welding (C)/No error (D). *(CDS 2002-II)*
10. One of the important benefits (A)/of machine age (B)/is that our standard of living has improved (C)/No error (D).

Exercise 58

1. This is the second communication we have sent (A)/and we are much surprised (B)/at receiving no answer (C)/No error (D).
2. Several guests noticed Mr. Sharma (A)/falling back in his chair (B)/and gasping for breath (C)/No error (D). *(CDS 2003-I)*
3. Long life is good (A)/if one be happy (B)/and has friends (C)/ No error (D).
4. His assistants have and are still doing (A)/excellent work for the organisation (B)/ No error (C). *(CDS 2003-I)*
5. None of the diplomats at the conference (A)/was able either (B)/to comprehend or to solve the problem (C)/No error (D).
6. Rather than go (A)/with Amit, he (B)/decided to stay at home (C)/No error (D).
7. He always practices (A)/the justice and (B)/cares for moral principles (C)/No error (D).
8. The whole block of flats (A)/including two shops were (B)/ destroyed in fire (C)/ No error (D). *(CDS 2003-I)*
9. He feels his troubles (A)/as much or (B)/even more than they (C)/No error (D).
10. Such rules (A)/do not apply to (B)/you and I (C)/No error (D).

Exercise 59

1. Teacher repeatedly warned the students (A)/not make a noise (B)/but the students did not obey (C)/No error (D). *(CDS 2003-II)*
2. My left leg has just been operated by (A)/a surgeon in (B)/Lohia hospital (C)/No error (D).
3. Teaching in this school would certainly improve (A)/if it had less boys (B)/in all the higher classes (C)/No error (D). *(CDS 2003-II)*
4. In some ways, the Diwali festival corresponds with Christmas (A)/ which is celebrated with enthusiasm by the Christians (B)/all over the world (C)/No error (D).
5. The expert mason reported the contractor (A)/that there was no question (B)/of the wall's falling down (C)/No error (D). *(CDS 2003-II)*
6. He went on committing crime after crime (A)/but in spite of my best efforts (B)/I could not prevent him to do so (C)/No error (D).

7. The population of Kolkata (A)/is greater than Delhi (B)/although Delhi is the capital of India (C)/No error (D). ***(CDS 2003-II)***
8. Though he denied his involvement in the case (A)/the facts made it clear (B)/that he had hand in the cruel murder of his friends (C)/No error (D).
9. The police (A)/has arrested (B)/four smugglers in Mumbai and Delhi (C)/No error (D).
10. Scarcely we had left the hotel (A)/when the thunderstorm burst (B)/over our heads (C)/No error (D).

Exercise 60

1. Her clothes (A)/were spattered (B)/by mud (C)/No error (D). ***(CDS 2004-I)***
2. He was beside (A)/himself with rage (B)/when he saw the mess (C)/No error (D).
3. We have benefitted from (A)/the discoveries bequeathed at us (B)/by the scientists of the last century (C)/No error (D). ***(CDS 2004-I)***
4. Although she didn't mention me by name (A)/I know her remarks (B)/were intended for my benefit (C)/No error (D).
5. He wasn't (A)/just unconsiderate (B)/he was downright rude (C)/ No error (D).
6. She's a bit (A)/of a doubting Thomas (B)/she won't believe you're back till she sees you (C)/No error (D). ***(CDS 2004-I)***
7. There were gasps of horror from (A)/the spectators as he (B)/fell from the tight rope (C)/No error (D). ***(CDS 2004-I)***
8. This drug should (A)/only be taken (B)/with the supervision of a doctor (C)/No error (D).
9. Different words with the (A)/same spelling are distinguished (B)/in this dictionary by a superscript number (C)/No error (D).
10. I won't go into all the depressing details (A)/let it suffice it to say that the (B)/whole affair was an utter disaster (C)/No error (D).

Exercise 61

1. Despite of a good monsoon this year (A)/the production of foodgrains in the country (B)/did not go up (C)/No error (D).
2. The last of the Mughal Emperors of India (A)/was first imprisoned and (B)/was later sent into exile by the British (C)/No error (D).
3. Hardly as I stepped out of my house (A)/when I saw some policemen (B)/coming towards my house (C)/No error (D). ***(CDS 2004-II)***
4. Today, the cost of living (A)/is such higher that many people (B)/ find it difficult to keep their hearth burning (C)/No error (D). ***(CDS 2004-II)***
5. Rina was trying for admission in the Engineering College (A)/even though her parents (B)/wanted her to take up medicine (C)/No error (D). ***(CDS 2004-II)***

6. Yavanika is one of the latest (A)/addition to good drama (B)/which appeared in recent times (C)/No error (D).
7. Children visiting the park (A)/are amused by the monkeys (B)/play in the cages (C)/No error (D). ***(CDS 2004-II)***
8. I am better acquainted (A)/with the country (B)/than you are (C)/No error (D).
9. Being occupied with important matters (A)/he had no leisure (B)/to see us (C)/ No error (D). ***(CDS 2004-II)***
10. He was not promoted to the (A)/rank of a Colonel (B)/till for a few months of his resignation (C)/No error (D).

Exercise 62

1. No student is (A)/as intelligent (B)/as my son (C)/No error (D). ***(CDS 2005-I)***
2. The most important feature (A)/of our products are that (B)/they are developed in-house (C)/No error (D).
3. When he was tired (A)/he took rest under (B)/the shade of a tree (C)/No error (D). ***(CDS 2005-I)***
4. The Principal along (A)/with the students (B)/have gone to Shimla (C)/No error (D).
5. When you have gone (A)/through my book (B)/give the same to me (C)/No error (D). ***(CDS 2005-I)***
6. He said a number of lies (A)/and then went without (B)/saying me good bye (C)/ No error (D).
7. Not only we saw (A)/the Education Minister but (B)/also the Chief Minister (C)/ No error (D). ***(CDS 2005-I)***
8. I came directly (A)/to my residence (B)/from the airport (C)/No error (D). ***(CDS 2005-I)***
9. I signed on the receipt (A)/in the morning but the pay (B)/has not been disbursed to me so far (C)/No error (D).
10. This is the same story (A)/which I heard (B)/from him yesterday (C)/No error (D). ***(CDS 2005-I)***

Exercise 63

1. There would be fewer follies (A)/and happiness and good feeling all around (B)/if we applied the scientific attitude for all our affairs (C)/ No error (D). ***(CDS 2000)***
2. Meera told to the teacher (A)/that she couldn't come for the rehearsals (B)/the next day (C)/No error (D).
3. I am told that Anjali has been (A)/suffering from fever (B)/since ten days (C)/No error (D).
4. The armed forces have been working around the clock (A)/to bring a semblance of normality (B)/in the flood-affected areas (C)/ No error (D). ***(CDS 2000)***

5. Just when Alfred Nobel's discoveries were beginning to get him rewards (A)/ which were to make him one of the richest man of his days (B)/an anti-Noble campaign was started in France (C)/ No error (D). *(CDS 2000)*
6. There is no definite rule (A)/regarding the length of a precis (B)/with relation to that of the original passage (C)/No error (D).
7. You had better hurry up (A)/if want to get home (B)/before dark (C)/No error (D).
8. When I shall get back (A)/I shall pay off the money (B)/that I borrowed from you last month (C)/No error (D).
9. A music and dance show have been organised (A)/to raise funds for the orphanage (B)/on the first Saturday of next month (C)/No error (D). *(CDS 2001)*
10. Both the boys (A)/came late in the hall (B)/and set besides me (C)/No error (D).

Exercise 64

1. Education helps us understand and tolerate differences (A)/and so holds out the promise (B)/that we can live together harmoniously (C)/No error (D). *(CDS 2001-II)*
2. He refused to disclose to his friends (A)/whether he will leave for England (B)/ immediately after finishing his studies (C)/ No error (D).
3. Despite of her protests (A)/I decided to buy (B)/the saree which she did not like (C)/No error (D). *(CDS 2001-II)*
4. The government warned the shop-keepers (A)/that if they persist in charging unfair prices (B)/their licences would be cancelled (C)/No error (D).
5. The famous poet and the scholar (A)/Dr. Suman has been ailing for (B)/the last one month (C)/No error (D).
6. All the animals (A)/including the zebras and the stags in the zoo (B)/ are sent to more colder places in the summer (C)/No error (D). *(CDS 2002)*
7. All the patients (A)/have been admitted (B)/and received careful attention (C)/ No error (D).
8. I cannot understand (A)/why does he not do the work (B)/as instructed (C)/No error (D). *(CDS 2002)*
9. There are several different attitudes (A)/that may be adopted (B)/for the spectacle of intolerable suffering (C)/No error (D).
10. Both of them (A)/help one another (B)/in the time of need (C)/ No error (D).

Exercise 65

1. There is sense of urgency (A)/in locating alternative source of water (B)/to augment the dwindling supply (C)/No error (D).
2. Although there is virtually no production in India (A)/the 'Encyclopedia Britannica' estimate (B)/that India has perhaps the largest accumulated stock of silver in the world (C)/No error (D). *(CDS 2002-II)*

3. Neither the severe earthquake (A)/or the subsequent famine (B)/could demoralise the people of the country (C)/No error (D).

4. As soon as I shall reach New Delhi (A)/I shall send you the file (B)/ you have asked for (C)/No error (D). *(CDS 2002-II)*

5. All the furnitures have been (A)/replaced by the owner of the house (B)/before shifting (C)/No error (D).

6. It is a (A)/quarter to ten (B)/by my watch (C)/No error (D). *(CDS 2003-I)*

7. I like reading (A)/more than (B)/to play games (C)/No error (D).

8. The sum and substance (A)/of this poem (B)/is as follows (C)/No error (D). *(CDS 2003-I)*

9. The team was (A)/now in the field and (B)/about to take their place (C)/No error (D).

10. Perhaps you know (A)/that I have passed (B)/the examination in 1990 (C)/No error (D). *(CDS 2003-I)*

Exercise 66

1. After a stay of several years abroad (A)/he has returned back (B)/to Delhi (C)/No error (D).

2. How can we break upon (A)/the barriers of fear and hostility (B)/ which divide the two communities ?(C)/No error (D). *(CDS 2003-I)*

3. Road accidents are so common now-a-days (A)/that many people (B)/give up their lives everyday (C)/No error (D).

4. The cricket match had called up (A)/at the last moment as the pitch had been dug up (B)/and oil had been poured on it (C)/No error (D).

5. It is incumbent (A)/with all the students (B)/to abide by the college rules (C)/No error (D).

6. I would not sullen (A)/my hands (B)/by accepting a bribe (C)/No error (D). *(CDS 2004-I)*

7. He gave her (A)/a suggestible glance (B)/and she blushed (C)/No error (D). *(CDS 2004-I)*

8. He unleashed (A)/a torrential of abuse (B)/against the unfortunate shop assistant (C)/No error (D).

9. There is (A)/unlikely (B)/to be rain (C)/No error (D).

10. The hotel room (A)/was bare (B)/and uninviting (C)/No error (D). *(CDS 2004-I)*

Exercise 67

1. The man who is perpetually (A)/hesitating which of the two (B)/he will do first, will ultimately do either (C)/No error (D). *(CDS 2004-II)*

2. No hill station is as (A)/beautiful as Darjeeling (B)/with its scenic beauties (C)/No error (D). *(CDS 2004-II)*

3. Being a well known Physicist (A)/he was invited to deliver (B)/a lecture on laser technology (C)/No error (D).

4. The chief idea of every common type (A)/of traveller is to see as (B)/many objects of interest as he possibly could (C)/No error (D).

5. He was hard down (A)/for money and was (B)/being harassed by his creditor (C)/No error (D). ***(CDS 2004-II)***

6. She's got (A)/a down at me (B)/I don't know why? (C)/No error (D).

7. What to speak of (A)/food even water (B)/was not available (C)/No error (D). ***(CDS 2005-I)***

8. It was difficult to get out (A)/because the street was full of people (B)/from one end to the another (C)/No error (D).

9. It had been our custom (A)/from time immemorial to be (B)/hospitable to those who come to our doors (C)/No error (D). ***(CDS 2005-I)***

10. She does not hardly (A)/know what (B)/happened yesterday (C)/No error (D).

Exercise 68

1. I began to suspect trouble (A)/as soon as one of the boys (B)/threw a stone at the policeman (C)/No error (D). ***(NDA 2001-I)***

2. It is all the more better (A)/for you to take the examination (B)/than to withdraw your form (C)/No error (D).

3. When a group of teenagers visited the entertainment centre (A)/little did they know (B)/that their outing will lead them to a hospital (C)/No error(D). ***(NDA 2001-I)***

4. If you had not been so secretive (A)/you had told me all the facts earlier (B)/I could have helped you (C)/No error (D).

5. Although there are some similarities (A)/in the qualification of both the candidates (B)/the differences among them are considerably pronounced (C)/No error (D). ***(NDA 2001-I)***

6. The king did not mind(A)/for putting the old people to death (B)/because he was young himself (C)/No error (D). ***(NDA 2001-I)***

7 In my opinion (A)/a pencil is always (B)/more preferable to a pen (C)/No error (D). ***(NDA 2001-II)***

8. It is harmful to sit close (A)/to the television set (B)/as it affects on the eyes (C)/No error (D). ***(NDA 2001-II)***

9. She soon lost her heart (A)/to her classmate (B)/and decided to become his life partner (C)/No error (D).

10. One of our subscriber (A)/reads four or five detective stories every week (B)/besides others which he gets from another library (C)/No error (D). ***(NDA 2001-II)***

Exercise 69

1. The elderly manager of the bank (A)/together with his staff (B)/have resigned (C)/No error (D). ***(NDA 2001-II)***
2. He served in this factory (A)/since it started (B)/after a long closure in 1960 (C)/ No error (D).
3. The hall was already packed (A)/and there was less room for the group of reporters (B)/who came to cover the event (C)/ No error (D).
4. We went to the zoo (A)/and had spent an enjoyable day (B)/looking at the various creatures there (C)/No error (D). ***(NDA 2002-I)***
5. It is else than (A)/his stupidity which stands (B)/in the way of his progress (C)/No error (D). ***(NDA 2002-I)***
6. Now that my children are grown up and gone out into the world (A)/I would like to spend my old age (B)/in the village I was born (C)/ No error (D).
7. When he persisted in making the same mistake (A)/despite constant reminders (B)/I explained him where he had gone wrong (C)/No error (D). ***(NDA 2002-I)***
8. The teacher asked me (A)/if I had done my homework (B)/and I replied in the negative (C)/No error (D). ***(NDA 2002-I)***
9. Every group of birds (A)/that fly the breeding ground (B)/will have an equal number of males and females (C)/No error (D).
10. Beware of (A)/a fair-weather friend (B)/who is neither a friend in need nor a friend indeed (C)/No error (D). ***(NDA 2002-II)***

Exercise 70

1. Copernicus proved (A)/that Earth (B)/moves round the Sun (C)/No error (D). ***(NDA 2002-II)***
2. Seldom we have been treated (A)/in such a rude manner (B)/by the police personnel (C)/No error (D). ***(NDA 2002-II)***
3. Some men are born great (A)/some achieve greatness (B)/and some had greatness thrust on them (C)/No error (D).
4. The property (A)/was divided (B)/among the two brothers (C)/No error (D).
5. I am quite certain (A)/that the lady is not only greedy (B)/but miserly (C)/No error (D). ***(NDA 2002-II)***
6. The aircraft was overloaded (A)/there was something wrong of the battery (B)/ and the engine was making a queer noise (C)/No error (D). ***(NDA 2003-I)***
7. A thorough inquiry of the misappropriation of funds (A)/is now imperative (B)/to bring the guilty to book (C)/No error (D).

8. His brilliant success in the examination (A)/as well as his record in sports (B)/ deserves high praise (C)/No error (D). ***(NDA 2003-I)***

9. While travelling by a train (A)/on a cold winter night (B)/an argument rose between two passengers in our compartment (C)/No error (D). ***(NDA 2003-I)***

10. I cannot find (A)/where has he gone (B)/though I have tried my best (C)/No error (D).

Exercise 71

1. Amit's severe bout of flu (A)/debilitated him so much (B)/that he was too tired to go for work for a week (C)/No error (D). ***(NDA 2003-II)***

2. This is the crux of the entire problem (A)/everything centres on (B)/it being resolved (C)/No error (D).

3. One of the major aims of the Air Force (A)/was the complete demolition of all means of transportation (B)/by the bombing of rail lines and terminals (C)/No error (D). ***(NDA 2003-II)***

4. His strong voice cut over (A)/the hum of conversation (B)/like a knife through butter (C)/No error (D).

5. Even though they weren't expecting us (A)/they managed to knock-up (B)/a marvellous meal (C)/No error (D). ***(NDA 2003-II)***

6. The celebrated singer was (A)/surrounded by the usual crowd (B)/of lackeys and hanger-ons (C)/No error (D).

7. If it weren't (A)/for you (B)/I wouldn't be alive today (C)/No error (D). ***(NDA 2004-I)***

8. He looked like a lion (A)/balked from (B)/its prey (C)/No error (D).

9. Widespread flooding (A)/is effecting (B)/a large area of the village (C)/No error (D). ***(NDA 2004-I)***

10. She regards (A)/negotiating prices with customers (B)/as her special preserve (C)/No error (D). ***(NDA 2004-I)***

Exercise 72

1. Often in political campaigns, a point is reached at which (A)/the candidates take out their gloves (B)/and start slugging with bare fists (C)/No error (D). ***(NDA 2004-I)***

2. If I was (A)/the Prime Minister of India (B)/I would have worked wonders (C)/No error (D). ***(NDA 2003-I)***

3. I pretended as if (A)/interested in the conversation (B)/but really it was very boring (C)/No error (D).

4. I don't usually like staying at hotels (A)/but last summer, we spent a few days (B)/ at a very nice hotel by sea (C)/No error (D).

5. I will try to be on time (A)/but do not worry (B)/when I am late (C)/No error (D). ***(NDA 2004-II)***

6. The teacher remarked that (A)/they all had (B)/done it very badly (C)/No error (D). ***(NDA 2004-II)***

7. The train is supposed (A)/to arrive at 10 AM yesterday (B)/but it was an hour late (C)/No error (D).

8. Ritu will be surprised (A)/as she hears (B)/the news (C)/No error (D). ***(NDA 2004-II)***

9. I asked two persons (A)/the way to the station (B)/but none of them knew it (C)/ No error (D).

10. Rajan told me that you had left (A)/the college a year before (B)/and looking for a job (C)/No error (D).

Exercise 73

1. The news of the disturbance (A)/was broadcasted (B)/on last Sunday (C)/No error (D).

2. Everyone visiting the house asked the young girl (A)/how could she kill the wolf (B)/single handed and without a weapon (C)/ No error (D).

3. While walking slowly in the park (A)/on a quiet summer afternoon (B)/a mad dog suddenly attacked him from behind (C)/No error (D).

4. Since the attachment of air-conditioned sleeping cars to all important trains. (A)/ travelling became very pleasant (B)/especially during the summer season (C)/No error (D).

5. It is the newspapers (A)/that exposes us to the widest range (B)/of human experiences and behaviour (C)/No error (D).

6. The method suggested in the lecture (A)/enables a student to learn more quickly (B)/and to have remembered for a longer period of time (C)/No error (D).

7. Last month we celebrated (A)/the wedding of our sister for whom (B)/we have been looking for suitable alliance for three years (C)/No error (D).

8. A leading textile manufacturer, one of the fastest growing in the industry (A)/is looking for a marketing manager (B)/to look up the marketing network of the company (C)/No error (D).

9. There was very heavy rain last night (A)/and the rivers have overflown their banks (B)/causing severe hardship to the people living by them (C)/No error (D).

10. Lock's treaties on government toleration and education (A)/show a mind fully awake in (B)/the possibilities of social reconstruction (C)/No error (D).

Exercise 74

1. Kamlesh asked the dealer (A)/what was the price (B)/of that bicycle and whether (C)/it is really made in Germany (D)/No error (E).

2. While luminaries of the dance world (A)/have no dearth of opportunity to display their art, (B)/the upcoming dancers suffer from (C)/an unfortunate lack of exposure (D)/No error (E).

3. Scarcely had I (A)/finished washing the car (B)/than the master came (C)/and asked me to clean the floor of the house (D)/ No error (E).

4. The job is much worse than I expected (A)/if I would have realised (B)/how awful it was going to be (C)/I would not have accepted it (D)/No error (E).

5. I am trying to finish (A)/this letter for the last one hour (B)/I wish you would (C)/ go away or stop disturbing me (D)/No error (E).

6. I offered him part-time work (A)/but he turned it over (B)/saying that he would (C)/rather wait for a full-time job (D)/No error (E).

7. He fixed a metal ladder (A)/for the wall below his window (B)/so as to be able to (C)/escape if there was a fire (D)/No error (E).

8. The foremost criteria of selection we adopted (A)/were the number of years of training (B)/a dancer had received (C)/under a particular guru (D)/No error (E).

9. He asked me (A)/if I am ill and (B)/I answered that I was not (C)/No error (D). ***(NDA 2005-I)***

10. The extraordinary ability of the satellites to (A)/see, listen and communicate has made them integral with (B)/modern warfare and nuclear war strategies in particular (C)/No error (D). ***(NDA 2005-I)***

Exercise 75

1. The principal of equal justice (A)/for all is one of (B)/the cornerstones of our (C)/ democratic way of life (D)/No error (E).

2. The Trust has succeeded (A)/admirably in raising (B)/money for (C)/future programmes (D)/No error (E).

3. Honesty, integrity and being intelligent (A)/are the qualities which (B)/we look for when (C)/we interview applicants (D)/ No error (E).

4. In order to save petrol, (A)/motorists must have to (B)/be very cautious (C)/ while driving along the highways (D)/No error (E).

5. If the by- stander had not been (A)/familiar with first- aid techniques, (B)/the driver which had met (C)/with the accident would have died (D)/No error (E).

6. None of the children (A)/has ever sang (B)/on any occasion (C)/in public before (D)/No error (E).

7. Neither the earthquake (A)/nor the subsequent fire (B)/were able to dampen (C)/the spirit of the residents (D)/No error (E).

8. The customer scarcely had (A)/enough money to pay (B)/to the cashier (C)/at the cash counter (D)/No error (E).

9. The apparently obvious solutions (A)/to most of his problems (B)/ were overlook by (C)/many of his friends (D)/No error (E).

10. By arresting the local criminals (A)/and encouraging good people (B)/we can end (C)/hostilities of that area (D)/No error (E).

11. The closure of the car factory (A)/had a knock-out effect (B)/on the tyre manufacturers (C)/No error (D). ***(NDA 2005-I)***

Exercise 76

1. Her and the (A)/other members of the group (B)/spoke to the person (C)/after their final victory (D).
2. In early India (A)/there has been very little to read (B)/except for the books sent (C)/from Britain (D).
3. Still remaining in the ancient castle (A)/are the Duke's collection of early Dutch paintings (B)/which will be (C)/donated to a museum (D).
4. Most students preferred (A)/courses in the classical arts to (B)/ courses in science unless (C)/they are science majors (D).
5. When she comes (A)/to see us (B)/she usually will bring (C)/some thing with her (D).
6. Why did you (A)/not told me (B)/that the meeting (C)/was postponed ? (D).
7. I did not want (A)/him to have spent (B)/all the money at (C)/the fair yesterday (D).
8. The assistant (A)/is never found (B)/wherever the manager (C)/want him (D).
9. He picked up (A)/the books (B)/and put it (C)/on the table (D).
10. They decided (A)/to talk it over (B)/at dinner (C)/No error (D).

Exercise 77

1. I am not hungry (A)/beside (B)/I do not like eggs (C).
2. Economics are (A)/now-a-days included as a subject (B)/in all colleges (C).
3. When he (A)/had got what (B)/he wanted (C)/he has gone home (D).
4. Of the two proposals (A)/we think (B)/the second is (C)/the most attractive (D).
5. If I wrote (A)/to my father now (B)/he will receive (C)/the letter tomorrow (D).
6. This road is (A)/worst than (B)/any other road (C)/of the city (D).
7. The driver as well as (A)/the conductor are (B)/responsible for this accident (C).
8. Some peoples (A)/feel that (B)/no progress is possible (C)/without discipline (D).
9. She told (A)/her mother that (B)/she is busy (C).
10. After listening to (A)/little of songs (B)/she switched off (C)/the radio (D).

Exercise 78

1. We erect monuments (A)/in the memory of great leaders (B)/lest their achievements (C)/might be forgotten (D).
2. He will not escape (A)/punishment unless (B)/he does not speak (C)/the truth (D).
3. Being a cold day (A)/neither my friend (B)/nor I was (C)/in a mood to go to market (D).
4. Such students (A)/who have not submitted (B)/their TC will not be allowed (C)/to appear in the examinations (D).
5. I went to the librarian and cashier (A)/and they gave me (B)/all facilities required (C)/to complete the project (D).
6. Milk is (A)/the most perfect (B)/food in the world (C).
7. What is there (A)/which is a secret (B)/between you and me (C).
8. By the death of Rajeev Gandhi (A)/a great statesman and politician (B)/were lost (C).
9. You had better (A)/to stop (B)/your work (C)/for some time (D).
10. A severe cold (A)/prevented the President (B)/being present (C)/at the function (D).

Exercise 79

1. I dislike (A)/my child (B)/watching TV (C)/all the time (D).
2. These people (A)/get their bath water (B)/from the river (C)/and their drink water from a well (D).
3. It was evident (A)/to me that there (B)/was any mistake (C)/in that account (D).
4. He does not seem (A)/to be aware (B)/as to (C)/his merits (D).
5. He declared (A)/at the top of his (B)/voice that (C)/it was not possible (D)/No error (E).
6. Crossing the road (A)/a car knocked (B)/him down (C).
7. The captain (A)/with all his team (B)/were held responsible (C).
8. Bangladesh has come (A)/into existence (B)/thirty years ago (C).
9. No sooner did (A)/she saw me (B)/than she came up (C)/and spoke to me (D).
10. No monument in the world (A)/is so beautiful (B)/as the Taj Mahal (C)/No error (D).

Exercise 80

1. Many a man (A)/have been (B)/working under me (C).
2. I told him (A)/the story (B)/in details (C)/to make him understand it fully (D).

3. Different authorities (A)/defines (B)/intelligence in different ways (C).

4. The old man (A)/told his sons (B)/that there was no such thing (C)/ like luck (D).

5. Everyone knows (A)/that the tiger (B)/is faster (C)/of all animals (D).

6. Sakshi wrote an essay (A)/so well that (B)/her teacher was (C)/very pleased with her (D).

7. The conference was (A)/attended (B)/by more than one hundred delegates (C)/ No error (D).

8. This is (A)/one of the most (B)/interesting book (C)/I have ever read (D).

9. Ram was happy (A)/that Rita and her sister was going (B)/by the same train (C)/ the next day (D).

10. The only criteria (A)/to judge (B)/a person (C)/is to observe his behaviour (D).

Exercise 81

1. No country can long endure (A)/if its foundations (B)/were not laid deep (C)/in the material prosperity (D).

2. Mahatma Gandhi did not solve (A)/all the future problems (B)/but he did solve (C)/problems of his own age (D).

3. We now look forward for (A)/some great achievements (B)/which to some extent (C)/can restore the country's prestige once again (D).

4. While Mahendra was away (A)/on a long official tour (B)/his office receive an important letter (C)/which was marked 'Urgent' (D).

5. We will pack not only (A)/the material properly (B)/but will also deliver it (C)/to your valued customers (D).

6. We cannot handle (A)/this complicated case today (B)/unless full details are not given (C)/to us by now (D).

7. According to one survey (A)/only those forests which were (B)/not under village management (C)/succumbed from fires recently (D).

8. Our school is making (A)/every possible effort (B)/to provide best facilities (C)/ and personal attention for each child (D).

9. We have done everything (A)/that could be done (B)/to avert the storm (C)/ which is now coming on (D)/No error (E).

10. Jayesh loved his Guru immensely (A)/and gave him fullest loyalty, (B)/yet he had his own (C)/independent way of thinking (D).

Exercise 82

1. This laboratory of physicists is (A)/not only equipped with (B)/all state-of-the-art instruments (C)/but also with outstanding physicists (D).

2. No method of making other (A)/people agree to (B)/your view point is (C)/as effective as this method (D).

3. I was pretty sure that (A)/he would support me (B)/for changing the age-old (C)/ and static structure of our organization (D).

4. I did not like his (A)/comments on my paper (B)/but I had no alternative (C)/as I had agreed to keep quiet (D)/No error (E).

5. The report is candid in admitting (A)/that the investment by the government (B)/ in health and family planning (C)/have eroded considerably (D).

6. He tried as he could (A)/but Naveen did not (B)/succeed in getting (C)/his car to start up (D).

7. Foolishly Madhu threw (A)/some water on the electric heater (B)/when it catches fire and (C)/she got a shock (D).

8. Rajesh was expecting (A)/a telegram from his uncle (B)/which would inform (C)/ him whether he went or not (D).

9. Either of the plans (A)/suits him and therefore (B)/he decided not to (C)/go out yesterday (D).

10. Inspite of the rumors (A)/of an impending takeover (B)/by the government, (C)/ Ramlal bought more shares of that company (D)/ No error (E).

Exercise 83

1. Our housing society comprises (A)/six block and thirty flats (B)/in an area of (C)/ about thousand square meters (D).

2. They took to (A)/reading times (B)/for better knowledge (C)/of the facts (D).

3. As I was to reach early (A)/I preferred train (B)/instead of (C)/bus (D).

4. He did not go (A)/to the city on foot (B)/he went there (C)/by the train (D).

5. One of the most (A)/widely spread (B)/bad habit (C)/is the use of tobacco (D).

6. Myself and Ramanujam (A)/will take care of (B)/the function (C)/on Saturday (D).

7. All the doctors (A)/were puzzled on the (B)/strange symptoms (C)/reported by the patient (D).

8. India is in no way (A)/inferior than the USA (B)/in the fertility of soil (C)/and richness of resources (D).

9. The visitors (A)/complained at (B)/the poor accommodation (C)/ they were given (D).

10. Amit's habit of (A)/delaying his work (B)/put his colleagues (C)/to a lot of trouble (D)/No error (E).

Exercise 84

1. Our housing society comprises of (A)/six blocks and thirty flats (B)/ in an area of (C)/about thousand square meters (D).
2. Not only the bandits robbed (A)/the traveller of his purse (B)/but also wounded him grievously (C).
3. The old woman has had the best medical facilities available (A)/but she will not be cured (B)/unless she does not have a strong desire to live (C).
4. Frozen foods are so popular today (A)/that many people wonder (B)/how they ever lived without them (C)/No error (D).
5. We should never be (A)/cent percent sure of our success (B)/in any walk of our life (C).
6. Smith including (A)/all the members of his family (B)/goes to the church every Sunday (C).
7. The students of now-a-days (A)/hesitate to talk (B)/to their teachers (C).
8. If you would have (A)/practised regularly (B)/you would have won the match (C).
9. Kanchenjungha is one of the (A)/beautiful peak (B)/of the (C)/Himalayan range (D).
10. He is one of the (A)/most intelligent (B)/student (C)/I have ever taught (D).

Exercise 85

1. Radha with (A)/her brothers (B)/and sisters (C)/are present here (D).
2. Men (A)/proposes (B)/but God (C)/disposes (D).
3. He gets (A)/up (B)/early at (C)/the morning (D).
4. The house (A)/is built (B)/in an (C)/attractive manner (D)/No error (E).
5. She worn (A)/a necklace (B)/studded (C)/with diamonds (D).
6. None (A)/of these (B)/students (C)/was there (D)/No error (E).
7. He (A)/was not (B)/blind (C)/from birth (D).
8. I said (A)/that a interesting (B)/face could (C)/also be pretty (D).
9. He love (A)/his father (B)/and his father (C)/also loved him (D).
10. Milking used (A)/to be a task (B)/or a duty cost (C)/on him (D).

Exercise 86

1. The doctor (A)/did not (B)/ask Mohan (C)/the time (D).
2. How do (A)/Vinoba appeal (B)/to the (C)/landlords (D)?
3. Bats are (A)/sometime seen (B)/in our (C)/houses (D).
4. I am glad (A)/Rex never saw (B)/a trained (C)/police dog jump (D).

5. His (A)/son met (B)/him (C)/on the door (D).
6. The plane (A)/was to (B)/take of (C)/at 6 AM (D).
7. This is (A)/our attitudes (B)/towards (C)/Ahimsa and Truth (D).
8. I caught him (A)/from the hand (B)/and began (C)/to plead (D).
9. We ought (A)/not to (B)/speak ill (C)/for others (D).
10. Radha works (A)/harder than (B)/I did (C)/her age (D).

Exercise 87

1. Krishna is (A)/the taller (B)/boy (C)/in the class (D).
2. Bhima was (A)/the man (B)/who all (C)/the Indians loved (D).
3. I can (A)/neither read (B)/or speak (C)/Hindi (D).
4. I have been (A)/suffering from (B)/fever since (C)/three days (D).
5. The committee (A)/is divided (B)/over (C)/this issue (D).
6. The Planning Commission expects (A)/the Gross Domestic Product to (B)/grow by a satisfactory (C)/rate during the year (D)/No error (E).
7. The language used for writing text books (A)/differs from other forms of writing (B)/in its preference on (C)/simplicity over style (D).
8. One of the basics of good writing (A)/is to have a (B)/clear understanding of the target audience (C)/and its requirements (D)/ No error (E).
9. This is an (A)/excellent site for (B)/a stadium which we (C)/should like to acquire (D).
10. If you absent (A)/from college, your (B)/name is likely to be (C)/ struck off the rolls (D).

Exercise 88

1. The man (A)/is (B)/a (C)/social animal (D).
2. Twenty five kilometers (A)/from Bhubaneshwar to Cuttack (B)/ are (C)/a long distance (D).
3. The institute (A)/imparts training (B)/in (C)/the French (D).
4. Looking forward (A)/to meet (B)/you (C)/soon (D).
5. Pass on (A)/the salt, (B)/please, (C)/do you (D)?
6. He is (A)/a mason (B)/who (C)/built my house (D).
7. I cannot (A)/make from (B)/what you are saying (C)/about him (D).
8. What (A)/you will think (B)/if school boys (C)/make fun of you (D) ?
9. The minister's speech (A)/has been reported (B)/to the newspaper (C)/No error (D).
10. No sooner (A)/we reached there (B)/then it started raining (C).

Exercise 89

1. Being a very cold day (A)/I would (B)/not go out for (C)/a morning walk (D).
2. Such an act of cruelty (A)/had never (B)/be committed (C)/before (D).
3. If you will (A)/insist upon (B)/challenging me, (C)/I will fight it out alone (D).
4. Fifty years (A)/have passed (B)/since (C)/Subhash Chandra Bose had died (D).
5. A good house (A)/and a good bank (B)/account is what (C)/he wants (D).
6. Of all the (A)/other teachers the (B)/students respected the history (C)/teacher the most (D).
7. He is one of those persons (A)/who listen (B)/to all advice but keep (C)/his own counsel (D).
8. No one but (A)/he knew (B)/who was (C)/setting the question paper (D)/No error (E).
9. A box (A)/of apples are (B)/in (C)/the car (D)/No errror (E).
10. The Principal threatened to (A)/inform to (B)/his father about (C)/his misdeeds (D).

Exercise 90

1. Sharad was entrusted with (A)/the task of co-ordination yesterday (B)/but due to certain difficulties (C)/he does not do it (D).
2. One should make (A)/his best efforts if (B)/one wishes to achieve (C)/success in this organization (D).
3. Having deprived from their (A)/homes in the recent earthquake (B)/they had no other option but (C)/to take shelter in a school (D).
4. The technician reminded (A)/them to have a (B)/throughly cleaning of the (C)/machine after use (D).
5. The villager told (A)/us where was the (B)/temple and even led (C)/us to the spot (D).
6. The person who (A)/they are referring (B)/to is none other (C)/than my close friend (D).
7. Mahesh was kind enough (A)/to inform us about the (B)/conspiracy but declined to (C)/name the person behind it (D)/No error (E).
8. He told the policeman (A)/that he would rather (B)/starve to stealing to get (C)/what he had been aspiring for (D).
9. In spite of the workload yesterday (A)/Nitin manages to play (B)/it cool and continued (C)/with his work as usual (D).
10. The demand of the workers' (A)/union that the dismissed (B)/employee to reinstated, has (C)/been accepted by the management (D).

Exercise 91

1. Thinking that he has finally found (A)/someone with similar interests, (B)/the scholar tried to strike up a conversation. (C)/No error (D).
2. Earlier this year, (A)/Constantan had entered the news via a video-tapted interview (B)/telecasted by commercial television channel. (C)/No error (D).
3. If you permit me to speak the truth, (A),/I shall say without hesitation (B)/that you have done a mistake (C)/No error (D).
4. My friend is so rich that (A)/he is having six houses in Mumbai (B)/ and four in Pune, (C)/No error (D).
5. He asked me (A)/if I am ill (B)/and I answered that I was not (C)/No error (D).
6. He lost his new knife (A)/shortly after (B)/he bought it. (C)/No error (D).
7. The ultimate problem of Physics (A)/is to reduce matter by analysis (B)/to its lowest condition or divisibility (C)/No error (D).
8. By the time (A)/she finished typing (B)/it was not hardly ten (C)/No error (D).
9. He like (A)/his companions (B)/were deceived (C)/No error (D).
10. He told me that you had left the school (A)/a year ago (B)/and seeking for a job (C)/No error (D).

Exercise 92

1. As I prefer coffee than tea (A)/my friends always take the trouble (B)/ to get a cup of coffee, whenever I visit them (C)/No error (D).
2. There has been (A)/little change in the patient's condition (B)/since he was moved to the special ward (C)/No error (D).
3. The king was perturbed (A)/to found evidence (B)/against his own queen (C)/No error (D).
4. They begged her (A)/not to go but she was determined (B)/and left the castle (C)/No error (D).
5. They cook meal, (A)/lay the table, (B)/clean the house and iron the clothes (C)/ No error (D).
6. No sooner did (A)/the doctor enter the house (B)/then the patient died (C)/No error (D).
7. The drawing room was a mess (A)/with all the furnitures (B)/scattered in total disarray (C)/No error (D).
8. The gap between what he preaches (A)/and what he practises is too wide (B)/to be accepted by anyone (C)/No error (D).
9. While flying over India (A)/we had glimpses of the two sources of her culture (B)/Ganges and Himalayas (C)/No error (D).
10. This picture (A)/is the best (B)/of the two (C)/No error (D).

Exercise 93

1. Finishing the work (A)/he was allowed to take rest (B)/for half an hour (C)/No error (D).
2. The pirates, who had hidden the treasure on the island, (A)/went back again (B)/ because they thought they can now remove it with safety (C)/No error (D).
3. In those early days (A)/the West paid lip-service (B)/to United Nations (C)/No error (D).
4. Ten Shillings (A)/was charged (B)/by him for the service (C)/No error (D).
5. To an amusing degree (A)/he was addicted to read the jokes in punch aloud (B)/ even when he was alone (C)/No error (D).
6. Why not stop the first man you meet next and ask, (A)/"could you tell me (B)/ what the time is" (C)/No error (D).
7. The invention of the internal combustion engine (A)/is considered to be (B)/a most unique development (C)/No error (D).
8. Put off (A)/the fire (B)/quickly (C)/No error (D).
9. A fight (A)/took place (B)/on the board of the ship. (C)/ No error (D).
10. Hardly the rains started (A)/when a child in the corner (B)/sent out a piercing wail (C)/No error (D).

Exercise 94

1. Don't think you can say unpleasant things (A)/about someone behind his back (B)/and not found out (C)/No error (D).
2. The Americans speak (A)/different from us (B)/though our grammar is the same (C)/No error (D).
3. This is an instance (A)/of the blind (B)/leading the blinds (C)/No error (D).
4. He took to drink (A)/to lessen (B)/his mental worries (C)/No error (D).
5. My father could lead (A)/a full and happy life (B)/without spending lot of money (C)/No error (D).
6. All India Radio broadcasted (A)/a very good programme (B)/this morning (C)/No error (D).
7. There were so much cattle (A)/on the road that (B)/it was difficult to drive safely (C)/No error (D).
8. What, could have provoked him to behave (A)/in such a rude manner (B)/at dinner last night (C)/No error (D).
9. They were rich zamindars in the thirties (A)/but now they have fallen on the evil days (B)/and have lost much of their property (C)/ No error (D).
10. The foreign ambassador was (A)/both noted for his charming manners (B)/as well as his wide knowledge of languages (C)/No error (D).

Exercise 95

1. The news of the disturbance (A)/was broadcasted (B)/the same evening (C)/No error. (D)
2. Everyone visiting the house asked the young girl (A)/how could she kill the wolf (B)/single handed and without a weapon (C)/ No error (D).
3. While walking slowly in the park (A)/on a quiet summer afternoon (B)/a mad dog suddenly attacked him from behind (C)/ No error (D).
4. Since the attachment of air-conditioned sleeping cars to all important trains (A)/ travelling became very pleasant (B)/especially during the summer season (C)/No error (D).
5. It is the newspapers (A)/that exposes us to the widest range (B)/of human experiences and behaviour (C)/No error (D).
6. The method suggested in the lecture (A)/enables a student to learn more quickly (B)/and to have remembered for a longer period of time (C)/No error (D).
7. Last month we celebrated (A)/the wedding of our sister for whom (B)/we have been looking for suitable alliance for three years (C)/No error (D).
8. A leading textile manufacturer, one of the fastest growing in the industry (A)/is looking for a marketing manager (B)/to look up the marketing network of the company (C)/No error (D).
9. There was very heavy rain last night (A)/and the rivers have over-flown their banks (B)/causing severe hardship to the people living by them (C)/No error (D).
10. The government warned the shopkeepers (A)/that if they persist in charging unfair prices (B)/their licences would be cancelled (C)/No error (D).

Exercise 96

1. The flicker of light from the gas lamps (A)/indicated that the night (B)/was barely passed (C)/No error (D).
2. India was committed to keep maintaining peace (A)/and solving all outstanding problems (B)/with her neighbours through dialogue (C)/No error (D).
3. Being the second Saturday of the month, (A)/he got up late and spent the whole day at home, (B)/doing his share of the household chores (C)/No error (D).
4. As economic restructuring in Central and Eastern Europe progresses, (A)/an estimated 15 million people may be out of work (B)/by the end of the year (C)/No error (D).
5. Such of those who have not paid the fees, (A)/the circular says, (B)/will not be permitted to attend classes (C)/No error (D).
6. There is a good British library in the city (A)/and anyone interested in books (B)/ can avail of the facility (C)/No error (D).

7. Those who are excessively careful (A)/for their health (B)/are not generally healthy (C)/No error (D).
8. Once we have agreed on (A)/the fundamentals, there will hardly be (B)/anything left to discuss about, (C)/No error (D).
9. I did ask him (A)/where you were (B)/but he didn't tell me, (C)/No error (D).
10. I will wait for you (A)/at the office (B)/till you will finish your work, (C)/No error (D).

Exercise 97

1. We had swam (A)/across the river (B)/before (C)/sunset. (D)/No error (E). ***(SBI PO Exam)***
2. Madhuri is (A)/more prettier (B)/than her (C)/younger sister. (D)/No error (E). ***(SBI PO Exam)***
3. A cell (A)/is the smallest (B)/identifiable unit of life and cannot be (C)/seen with a naked eye (D)/No error (E). ***(IIT Kharagpur)***
4. If a student needs advices about (A)/careers, (B)/he or she should consult (C)/the Career officer (D)/No error (E). ***(IIT Kharagpur)***
5. Had they have been in (A)/my condition, (B)/they would have felt (C)/miserable and thought of committing suicide. (D)/No error (E). ***(RRB Kolkata)***
6. The Secretary of the worker's union (A)/remarked that the present government is so selfish (B)/that it cared very little (C)/about solving anyone else's problem (D)/No error (E). ***(RRB Kolkata)***
7. He don't know (A)/the difference between (B)/a ship and a submarine (C)/No error (D). ***(SSC Clerical Exam)***
8. Yesterday I met an old friend (A)/when I are going (B)/to the market (C)/No error (D). ***(SSC Clerical Exam)***
9. Cattles (A)/were grazing (B)/in the meadows (C)/near our farm (D)/No error (E). ***(BSRB Clerical Exam)***
10. You are really (A)/senior than (B)/me (C)/in age (D)/No error (E). ***(BSRB Clerical Exam)***

Exercise 98

1. Make haste (A)/lest (B)/you should not miss (C)/the train (D)/No error (E). ***(BSRB Clerical Exam)***
2. Many of us (A)/do not know (B)/to swim (C)/at all (D)/No error (E). ***(BSRB Clerical Exam)***
3. His car is (A)/more bigger than (B)/that of any of us (C)/No error (D). ***(SSC Clerical Exam)***
4. One of my uncles (A)/is a doctor (B)/in America (C)/No error (D). ***(SSC Clerical Exam)***

5. This machine looks (A)/good but is very (B)/badly designed (C)/and doesn't work good (D)/No error (E). ***(IIT Kharagpur)***

6. He is well-known for both (A)/his kindness (B)/as well as (C)/his understanding (D)/No error (E). ***(IIT Kharagpur)***

7. Ramu closely (A)/resembles to his father (B)/not only in physical features (C)/but also in habits (D)/No error (E). ***(SBI PO Exam)***

8. After he had read the two first chapters (A)/of the novel (B)/he felt like reading (C)/the book at one sitting (D)/No error (E). ***(SBI PO Exam)***

9. India is (A)/one of the leading (B)/film producing country (C)/in the world (D)/No error (E). ***(CSRB Patna Exam)***

10. Hardly had (A)/I left the house (B)/then it began (C)/to rain (D)/No error (E). ***(CSRB Patna Exam)***

Exercise 99

1. He told me (A)/that he wrote a letter (B)/to his superior (C)/for a certain reason (D)/No error (E). ***(BSRB Clerical Exam)***

2. The teacher told the boys (A)/that one (B)/ought to work hard (C)/ to earn one living (D)/No error (E). ***(BSRB Clerical Exam)***

3. The obstacles to which (A)/Gandhiji had to surmount (B)/were mostly (C)/on the moral and spiritual grounds (D)/No error (E). ***(BSRB)***

4. Unless you do not (A)/take care of your health (B)/you will continue (C)/to suffer (D)/No error (E). ***(BSRB)***

5. After Ravi (A)/read the (B)/magazines and newspapers, and watched the TV programme, he decided (C)/to go out and meet some old friends (D)/No error (E). ***(RRB Kolkata)***

6. Everyone agrees that (A)/the Ganga is the holiest (B)/of all other rivers (C)/of India (D)/No error (E). ***(BSRB Bhopal)***

7. The issues are (A)/complex and (B)/has been obscured (C)/by other factors (D)/No error (E). ***(CSRB Patna)***

8. The bus was (A)/hired by (B)/the ladies (C)/for its picnic (D)/No error (E). ***(CSRB Patna)***

9. If (A)/it snowed tomorrow (B)/we'll go (C)/skating. (D)/No error (E). ***(SBI PO)***

10. A quarrel arose between the five members (A)/and for a time (B)/it appeared as if the party (C)/had been heading for a split (D)/No error (E). ***(SBI PO)***

Exercise 100

1. They had swam (A)/across the river (B)/before (C)/the sun sets (D)/No error (E). ***(SBI PO)***

2. She is (A)/more prettier (B)/than her (C)/friend Sheela (D)/No error (E). ***(SBI PO)***

3. Everyone of (A)/the staff members present here (B)/has given a day's pay (C)/as their contribution to the fund. (D)/No error (E). ***(CSRB Patna)***

4. Found guilty (A)/on murder (B)/the accused was (C)/sentenced to death (D)/No error (E). ***(CSRB Patna)***

5. The criminal was (A)/sentenced to death (B)/and was hung for his crime (C)/No error (D). ***(SSC Clerical)***

6. He said that (A)/he will help me (B)/secure a decent job (C)/No error (D). ***(SSC Clerical)***

7. The recent symposium on censorship (A)/indicated that to refrain with saying or writing (B)/something, others might object (C)/to, is a form of self-censorship (D)/No error (E). ***(RRB Kolkata)***

8. The Indian way (A)/of thinking is superior (B)/to most of the (C)/ countries of the world (D)/No error (E). ***(RRB Kolkata)***

9. I am certain that none (A)/of these two books (B)/is useful to the (C)/students of the 8th standard (D)/No error (E). ***(BSRB Lucknow)***

10. The lawyer asked me (A)/where had I (B)/kept clothes (C)/before taking a dip in the river (D)/No error (E). ***(BSRB Lucknow)***

Exercise 101

1. Like most young (A)/women living at homes, I can't really (B)/talk about my ideas or what I really feel, to my parents. (C)/No error (D).

2. The minister conferred (A)/with his colleagues (B)/and agreed that the new projects on education (C)/should be sanctioned immediately (D)/No error (E). ***(RRB Kolkata)***

3. Sunil is (A)/a best student (B)/in our class (C)/at present. (D)/No error (E). ***(CSRB Patna)***

4. It is in 1929 (A)/that we first (B)/flew to (C)/the United States (D)/ No error (E). ***(CSRB Patna)***

5. Being a (A)/fine day we went out (B)/for picnic (C)/at Okhla (D)/ No error (E). ***(BSRB Clerical)***

6. Many a man (A)/have been (B)/working (C)/under me (D)/No error (E). ***(BSRB Clerical)***

7. Please explain to me (A)/how is a digital computer (B)/different from (C)/an analog computer (D)/No error (E). ***(IIT Kharagpur)***

8. I'll work for you (A)/as long as (B)/you'll pay (C)/well (D)/No error (E). ***(IIT Kharagpur)***

9. Had you informed me earlier (A)/I would have (B)/certainly purchase (C)/the car for you (D)/No error (E). ***(BSRB Lucknow)***

10. It was seven o'clock (A)/in the evening that (B)/the train steamed (C)/into the station (D)/No error (E). ***(CSRB Patna)***

Exercise 102

1. Even if he had been driving more slowly (A)/it will have been quite impossible (B)/to avoid the accident (C)/No error (D). ***(Investigators Ex)***
2. Would you please (A)/stop from smoking (B)/while the ceremony (C)/is in progress (D)/No error (E). ***(Investigators Ex)***
3. When I offered him to help (A)/which he needed, (B)/he persisted in refusing it (C)/so I left him to his fate (D)/No error (E). ***(BSRB Clerical)***
4. He reminded me (A)/that he has (B)/often told me not to (C)/play with fire (D)/ No Error (E). ***(BSRB Clerical)***
5. Our country need (A)/a number of (B)/self sacrificing and (C)/devoted political leaders (D)/No error (E). ***(CSRB Patna)***
6. Instead of (A)/his busy and hard life (B)/he still retains (C)/freshness and robustness (D)/No error (E). ***(CSRB Patna)***
7. The smuggler yielded (A)/for the temptation (B)/and fell into (C)/the police trap (D)/No error (E). ***(CSRB Patna)***
8. The girl said (A)/that she preferred (B)/the blue gown (C)/than the black one (D)/No error (E). ***(CSRB Patna)***
9. Of the two principles (A)/he put forward, the last one (B)/was the more (C)/ difficult to understand (D)/No error (E). ***(IIT Kharagpur)***
10. All of us (A)/surprised (B)/to see an old man of (C)/sixty taking part in the Marathon held last month (D)/No error (E). ***(IIT Kharagpur)***

Example 103

1. The new railway line will greatly improve (A)/transport and communication (B)/ in eastern part of the country (C)/No error (D). ***(SSC Clerical)***
2. The receptionist asked me (A)/who do I want (B)/to meet in the office. (C)/No error (D). ***(SSC Clerical)***
3. At last (A)/he was married (B)/with a poor girl (C)/No error (D). ***(BSRB Clerical)***
4. She said (A)/that she will help me (B)/whenever I was in difficulty (C)/No error (D). ***(BSRB Clerical)***
5. Neither Rakesh (A)/nor I are leaving (B)/for Hyderabad (C)/No error (D). ***(SBI PO)***
6. Death (A)/is preferable (B)/than life (C)/No error (D). ***(SBI PO)***
7. We were still talking (A)/about what we should do (B)/when we heard (C)/the children shouting (D)/No error (E). ***(BSRB Clerical)***
8. As soon as the peon rings (A)/the first bell (B)/then all the students assemble (C)/ on the playground for prayer. (D)/No error (E). ***(BSRB Clerical)***

9. Have you (A)/turned detective (B)/that you keep your eye (C)/on me like this (D)/No error (E). *(BSRB Clerical)*

10. She asked him (A)/what it was that made him (B)/so much stronger and braver (C)/than any man (D)/No error (E). *(BSRB Clerical)*

Exercise 104

1. Being he (A)/is interested in getting himself examined (B)/by a heart specialist (C)/we must try our best to take him to a reputed doctor (D)/No error (E). *(RRB Kolkata)*
2. The college is (A)/holding special lectures for their students (B)/and teachers so that they (C)/may get enlightened about the economic problems (D)/No error (E). *(RRB Kolkata)*
3. A cell (A)/is the smallest (B)/identifiable unit of life and cannot be (C)/seen with a naked eye (D)/No error (E). *(IIT Kharagpur)*
4. If he needs advices about (A)/career, (B)/he should consult (C)/ the career officer (D)/No error (E).
5. Being a (A)/rainy day we went out (B)/for a picnic (C)/to Nehru Kendra (D)/No error (E). *(BSRB Clerical)*
6. Many a man (A)/have been (B)/participating (C)/in the competition (D)/No error (E). *(BSRB Clerical)*
7. To our surprise (A)/we noticed that (B)/every soldier and every sailor (C)/was in his place (D)/No error (E). *(BSRB Lucknow)*
8. Neither he nor I (A)/was able to (B)/finish the task within (C)/the time limit (D)/ No error (E). *(BSRB Lucknow)*
9. No sooner we entered (A)/than he got up (B)/and left the room (C)/ No error (D). *(SSC Clerical)*
10. The villagers fled away their houses (A)/when they saw (B)/the flood water rising (C)/No error (D). *(SSC Clerical)*

Exercise 105

1. I know (A)/he is having (B)/a lot of books (C)/on how to improve English (D)/No error (E). *(IIT Kharagpur)*
2. The theory of relativity is (A)/so complicated (B)/as we cannot describe (C)/it in a few sentences (D)/No error (E). *(IIT Kharagpur)*
3. After the brief appearence before the waiting crowds, (A)/he was taken (B)/to the Governor chamber (C)/for the swearing in ceremony (D)/No error (E). *(RRB Kolkata)*
4. Congress dissidents and (A)/a wide range among the (B)/opposition has mounted a (C)/campaign to have the President renominated (D)/No error (E). *(RRB Kolkata)*

5. If I would have (A)/worked regularly (B)/I would have passed (C)/the examination (D)/No error (E). *(CSRB Patna)*

6. The gentleman (A)/together with his (B)/wife and daughter (C)/ were drowned (D)/No error (E). *(CSRB Patna)*

7. No man (A)/in our country (B)/is as rich (C)/as he is (D)/No error (E). *(BSRB Clerical Bhopal)*

8. The teacher remarked (A)/very angrily yesterday (B)/that the boys have (C)/all done it very badly (D)/No error (E). *(BSRB Clerical Bhopal)*

9. A letter of recommendation (A)/from the Principal and (B)/the head of English department have helped him to (C)/get this lucrative job (D)/No error (E). *(BSRB Clerical Bhopal)*

10. An Indian driver or carpenter has to work (A)/about two hours to buy kilogram of rice (B)/while his counterparts in Austria, the Netherlands and Switzerland (C)/ need work only fifteen minutes for it (D)/No error (E). *(Rly. REE Kolkata)*

Exercise 106

1. The vehicle which is stopped (A)/by the policeman (B)/contained a number (C)/of smuggled watches (D)/No error (E). *(BSRB Lucknow)*

2. One should look for his (A)/own faults first (B)/and then those (C)/of others (D)/ No error (E). *(BSRB Lucknow)*

3. Sitting under the shade (A)/of a tree for a while (B)/made us fresh (C)/for the further journey (D)/No error (E). *(BSRB Lucknow)*

4. Although it is summer (A)/yet the weather at the (B)/hill station was (C)/quite pleasant (D)/No error (E). *(BSRB Lucknow)*

5. The smuggler yielded (A)/for the temptation (B)/and fell into (C)/ the police trap (D)/No error (E). *(CSRB Patna)*

6. The girl said (A)/that she preferred (B)/the blue gown (C)/than the black one (D)/No error (E). *(CSRB Patna)*

7. Cattles (A)/were grazing (B)/in the meadows (C)/near our farm (D)/No error (E). *(BSRB Clerical)*

8. You are really (A)/senior than (B)/me (C)/in age (D)/No error (E). *(BSRB Clerical)*

SOLUTIONS

Exercise 1

1. (C) Here 'a' is used with elephant instead of 'an'. An elephant is correct.
2. (B) It is a most beautiful painting. Use 'the' before 'most', being Superlative.
3. (E) No error.
4. (C) I go to **the** cinema every Sunday.
5. (C) Replace 'a' by 'an'. Here 'an' will be used instead of 'a' because 'h' is silent.
6. (C) He always speaks 'the' truth.
7. (A) The Kashmiri shawls. 'The' is used before noun which name the inhabitants of a country or city collectively.
8. (D) Delete 'The' before Agra, being proper noun.
9. (A) The Bible said. 'The' is used before the names of renowned books of religion or literature.
10. (A) A horse is running in the ground. 'A' is used with the singular countable noun which pronounced with the consonant sound.

Exercise 2

1. (A) 'A' European dish is very famous. Here 'European' begin with vowel 'E' even then its sounds 'yoo' or 'u'.
2. (E) 'A' is used with certain numerical terms to give the sense of 'one'. So, there is no error.
3. (C) Ritika helps 'the' poor and the sick people.
4. (A) Sapna is a very beautiful girl. 'The' is not used before proper noun.
5. (C) I saw a one rupee note on the road. 'A' is used with singular countable nouns pronounced with consonant sound.
6. (A) A boy is swimming on the pool. 'A' is used with the singular countable noun.
7. (A) Here is 'the' red shirt which Sapna gave me yesterday. Red shirt has become particularised.
8. (A) The Shatabdi Express. 'The' is used before the names of well-known trains.
9. (E) No error. 'The' is used before particular meals.
10. (C) My uncle is an S.P. Here, 'An' is used before a consonant which sounds like a vowel.

Exercise 3

1. (C) Gold is a useful metal. Before 'useful', we should put 'a' instead of 'an'.
2. (E) 'A' is used with positive and comparatives but not with superlatives.

3. (E) 'The' is used before a noun which is repeated after it has been introduced once.

4. (A) Punjabi 'The' is not used before name of the language.

5. (E) No error. 'The' is used with the superlative degree of adjective.

6. (D) In the east. 'The' is used with the name of 'directions' like east, west, north, south.

7. (E) 'The' is used with the professions like the nursing, the medical profession.

8. (A) Milk is good for health. 'The' article is omitted before proper nouns, material nouns, uncountables etc., in general.

9. (C) 'The' baby.

10. (D) Kunal was sent to prison. 'The' article is omitted before church, prison, hospital, college, school and bed, when the visit to these places is for the purpose they are primarily built .

Exercise 4

1. (E) 'The' Article is omitted before modes of transportation or travel. Always use by bus, by car, by train, etc.

2. (C) Insert 'the' before school. When the visit to places like school, church, hospital, prison are for the purpose other than they are primarily built , always use 'the' before these nouns.

3. (E) No error, 'The' is not used before name.

4. (A) Remove 'the' before 'Winters'. Do not use article before name of the seasons.

5. (A) Monkeys jumps on the trees. 'The' article is omitted before plural countable nouns when they tell about class or caste etc.

6. (E) 'The' is used before a singular countable noun meant to represent a whole class or kind.

7. (A) Insert 'The' before Chief Minister. Use 'the' before designation.

8. (C) Kshitiz is an honest boy. Here 'an' is used before a word beginning with silent 'H'.

9. (D) The sun rises in 'the' east is 'a' universal truth. 'A' is used before a word beginning with the sound 'u' (pronounced as 'yoo' or 'u').

10. (A) The 'Times of India' .... 'The' is used before the name of the newspapers and magazines.

Exercise 5

1. (E) No Error.

2. (A) Delete 'the' before Mahatma Gandhi. Article is not used before the name. (proper noun)

3. (A) The chinese .... 'The' is used before nationality.

4. (A) The Taj Mahal .... 'The' is used before the name of Monuments.

5. (C) 'The' is used before name of country UK, USA etc.

6. (C) My mothor is in the kitchen. Here 'The' is used before the noun which can be understood easily.

7. (B) The teacher called the last boy........... 'The' is used before the ordinals.

8. (A) An apple...... 'An' is used here before a word beginning with a vowel (a,e,i,o,u,) sound.

9. (E) 'The' will be used, with comparative to show that two things increase or decrease in the same proportion.

10. (E) Here 'the intelligent' means intelligent person and the 'duffers' means duffer persons.

11. (D) Shreya gave me a watch. 'A' is used before a word beginning with a consonant.

Exercise 6

1. (A) Delete 'the' before conclusion. The correct phrase is in conclusion.

2. (A) Replace 'the' by 'a'. In the question 'most' is not used as superlative.

   See the difference :

   (a) Sarla is the most beautiful girl in the college.

   (b) Sarla is a most beautiful girl.

3. (D) Use 'a' before turn.

4. (C) Delete 'the' before Mexico.

5. (C) Write 'the' before theatre. The correct phrase is go to the theatre go to the cinema.

6. (D) Delete 'the' before 'life'.

7. (D) Replace 'a' by 'an'.

8. (B) Write 'a' before 'good part'.

9. (C) Write 'a' before little.

10. (C) Delete 'the' before church.

Exercise 7

1. (C) Say 'died'. This is a question of past tense.

2. (A) Delete 'will' after 'when'. In such constructions don't 'will' after; when/as well as/until/after/as.

3. (A) Delete 'had'. In past perfect tense, simple past is used for the work completed later.

4. (C) Write 'I have' seen.

5. (A) Write 'whenever he comes'. For habitual action, present indefinite is used.

6. (B) Write 'he is teaching'.
7. (B) Write you 'started'.
8. (C) Delete 'will'. See explanation question no. 2.
9. (A) Write I cross.
10. (C) Write 'he gets up'.

Exercise 8

1. (B) Write 'have studied'. The sentence is in present tense.
2. (D) Write 'it hates'.
3. (A) Write 'it appears'.
4. (A) Write I have 'known'. Do not use progressive form with 'know'.
5. (A) Write 'If he had done this'. It is a conditional structure.
6. (B) Write 'had happened'. The sentence is in past.
7. (C) Write 'keep' it.
8. (D) Write I 'had expected'.
9. (A) Write I 'have' lived. The sentence is in present tense.
10. (A) Write, The chairman 'did not take'.
11. (A) Write 'They had got'.
12. (E) No error.
13. (A) Write I 'admire'. In general, know, admire, adore, trust, hope, rely are not used in progressive form.
14. (A) Write He 'has' been.
15. (D) Write is 'growing'.
16. (A) Write 'Here comes'. This is an exclamatory construction.
17. (B) Write 'She had told'. The sentence is in past.
18. (B) Write 'makes' instead of made.
19. (C) Write 'she has completed'.

Exercise 9

1. (A) Delete 'will' before the word 'find'.
2. (D) Write if it 'rained'. When reporting verb is in past, the reported speech will also be in past.
3. (B) Write 'she had'.
4. (B) Write 'will have reached'. This is a sentence of future perfect.
5. (C) Delete 'will' before 'get'.

6. (D) Write 'is growing'. The sentence is in present progressive.
7. (B) Write stopped, (Delete 'had')
8. (A) Write 'if I were'.
9. (D) Write 'keep'. The sentence is in present tense.
10. (B) Write what 'had' happened. The sentence is in past tense.

Exercise 10

1. (C) Write 'else's'. Use of apostrophe is necessary here.
2. (D) Write 'India's', to make the comparison logical.
3. (C) Write 'him' for 'his'. Use objective form pronoun before participle.
4. (A) Write 'questions' for 'question' remember to use plural noun after one of/one of the/ many of the.
5. (B) Write Ram and Sita's. One apostrophe will be used in such case.
6. (A) Write 'girl students' instead of 'girls student'.
7. (B) Replace 'two important informations' by 'two important pieces of information'.
8. (B) Delete 'a' before 'home work'. Home work is an uncountable noun.
9. (B) Replace 'two third' by 'two thirds'.
10. (A) Replace 'woman teachers' by 'women teachers'.
11. (D) Write 'rupee' for 'rupees'.
12. (B) Replace 'bricks' by 'pieces of brick'.
13. (B) Write two 'dozen' copies.
14. (C) Write 'hair' for 'hairs'. 'Hair' can't be usually pluralised by adding 's'.
15. (C) Replace 'whereabout' by 'whereabouts'. 'Whereabouts' means 'address'.

Exercise 11

1. (D) Replace 'itself' by 'themselves'. Here, Board of Director is not used as a collective noun.
2. (C) Replace 'their' by 'his'. Singular pronoun is used when two singular nouns are preceded by each/every.
3. (B) Replace 'themselves' by 'himself'. When two nouns are joined together with as well as/besides/in addition to, the pronoun is governed by the noun that comes first.
4. (C) Replace 'lazy one' by 'lazy ones'.
5. (B) Replace 'who' by 'that'. Remember to use 'that' after, all/none/some/only/other.

6. (A) Replace 'any' by 'either'. 'Either' is used for two.
7. (B) Replace 'whom' by 'who'.
8. (A) Write 'himself' after 'introduced'.
9. (D) Replace 'him' by 'he'. When two subjects are being compared, use pronoun in subjective case.
10. (B) Replace 'who' by 'that'.

Exercise 12

1. (A) Replace 'whomever' by 'whoever'.
2. (D) Replace 'each other' by 'one another'. 'Each other' is used for two.
3. (E) No error.
4. (D) Replace 'the same' by 'it'. 'The same' is used as an adjective, it should not be used as a pronoun.
5. (C) Replace 'I' by 'me'. Remember to use objective form pronoun after 'let'.
6. (C) Delete 'she'. The use of 'she' is unwarranted.
7. (C) Place 'it' after 'knows'.
8. (B) Replace 'laugh' by 'laughs'.
9. (A) Replace 'myself' by 'I'.
10. (D) Write 'it' after give. 'give' is a transitive verb, so it must have an object.

Exercise 13

1. (D) Write 'to' before 'do'.
2. (A) Say 'After taking breakfast' or Having taken breakfast. This is a question of dangling participle.
3. (C) Delete 'been'. Use of 'been' here is unwanted.
4. (A) Say 'while he was going towards the gate'. This is a question of dangling participle.
5. (B) Delete 'to' after 'nothing but'. Use of 'to' after 'nothing but' is incorrect.
6. (D) Delete 'to'. Use of 'to' after 'let' is incorrect.
7. (C) Delete 'to' before 'sing'. In such sentences, never use 'to' after; hear, see, make, know, feel.
8. (A) Use of 'Had' is wrong. Delete 'had'.
9. (B) Delete 'to'. Use of 'to' after 'than' is incorrect.
10. (B) Say 'forget her completely'. Splitting the infinitive here is not correct.

Exercise 14

1. (C) Delete 'into' after 'entered'.
2. (C) Delete 'to' after listening. If there is no object after listen, we should not use 'to'.
3. (A) Say apparent 'to'.
4. (A) Say proposed 'to'.
5. (C) Replace 'among' by 'between'. 'Between' is used for two.
6. (D) Say 'and about the poor'.
7. (C) Say 'blind in'.
   blind in left or right eye.
   blind of an eye.
   blind with both eye.
8. (B) Say 'amongst'.
9. (B) Use of 'with' is unnecessary.
10. (B) Say 'admits of'.

Exercise 15

1. (C) Say 'loss of'.
2. (D) Replace 'to' by 'for'.
3. (D) Say 'worthy of' instead of 'worthy for'.
4. (C) Delete 'on'.
5. (A) Say 'decline in' instead of 'decline of'.
6. (B) Delete 'for'. Order is a transitive verb, so it takes object without any preposition.
7. (B) Say 'on' land.
8. (C) Delete 'to' before 'Madras'.
9. (D) Use 'to' instead of 'for' after invited.
10. (C) Say look 'after' instead of 'for'.

Exercise 16

1. (A) Delete 'for' after await. 'Wait for' is correct, but 'await for' is incorrect.
2. (C) Say debarred 'from'. Use proposition 'from' after : debar/ abstain/refrain.
3. (A) Delete 'of' after 'despite'. Either say 'inspite of' or 'despite'.
4. (A) Say 'yielded to'.
5. (B) Say 'dying of hunger'.

6. (C) Replace ' rather than' by 'to'. After prefer/ senior/junior, use preposition 'to'.
7. (D) Replace 'by' by 'for'.
8. (C) Replace 'to stay in' by 'rather than stay in'.
9. (C) Say 'startled at'.
10. (B) Say 'free himself from'.

Exercise 17

1. (C) Replace 'that' by 'as'. The structure of the sentence is based on so ...... as.
2. (A) Say "He comes here not only for having lunch".
3. (C) Replace 'unless' by 'until' as 'until' is used in reference to time while 'unless' is used in reference to condition.
4. (C) Replace 'when' by 'of'. This is a conditional structure.
5. (B) Replace 'that' by 'since'.
6. (D) Replace 'as' by 'like'. 'As' is used with nominative and 'like' with objective pronoun.
7. (B) Replace 'along with the' by 'and'. The construction is Both.... and.
8. (D) Replace 'as' by 'like'.
9. (D) Replace 'than' by 'when'. Use 'when' with 'hardly'.
10. (D) Replace 'when' by 'than'. Use 'than' with 'No sooner'.

Exercise 18

1. (B) Replace 'and' by 'but'. There is a contrast in the sentence.
2. (A) Place 'not only' before 'to the rich'.
3. (B) Use of 'therefore' is superfluous.
4. (B) Replace 'since' by 'that'. 'Since/for' is usually used with perfect tense.
5. (B) Replace 'that' by 'whether'.
6. (D) Replace 'like him' by 'as he'.
7. (B) Replace 'ever' by 'never'.
8. (A) Replace 'or' by ' if'. Seldom if ever or seldom or never is possible.
9. (D) Replace 'would' by 'should'. After 'lest' use 'should'.
10. (B) Delete 'that'.
11. (C) Replace 'so' by 'as'. The construction so ... as is usually used in negative sentence and as ...... as in affirmative sentences.
12. (B) Replace 'if' by 'whether'. The structure is based in whether .... or.

13. (B) Replace 'which' by 'that'. Use 'that' with 'same'.

14. (C) Replace 'which' by 'as'.

15. (C) Delete 'so'. It is superfluous.

Exercise 19

1. (A) Change ' further' to 'farther'.
2. (A) Change 'smarter' to 'smart'. Use positive degree before 'enough'.
3. (B) Delete 'the most', before 'unique'. Unique, square, whole, full are used as superlative. Avoid using two superlative in sequence.
4. (B) Either write 'better' or 'comparatively good'.
5. (C) Replace 'more tall' by 'taller'.
6. (A) Replace 'A lots of' by 'lots of' or 'A lot of'.
7. (C) Write 'better' only. Avoid using two comparatives.
8. (B) Replace 'some' by 'any'.
9. (C) Replace 'more cold' by 'colder'.
10. (D) Replace 'more' by 'most'. For more than two things, use superlative.
11. (B) Change 'each and every' to ' each'. For two, use 'each'.
12. (A) Replace 'whole the' by 'the whole'.
13. (C) Replace 'last' by 'latest'.
14. (A) Replace 'than' by 'to'. After Junior/Senior/Prior, use preposition 'to'.
15. (C) Replace 'utmost' by 'outermost'.
16. (B) Replace 'much' by 'more'. The comparative of 'much' is 'more'.
17. (C) Replace 'first' by 'foremost'.

Exercise 20

1. (B) Replace 'we can' by 'can we'. This is a question of inversion.
2. (C) Use 'only' after 'died' to make the meaning logical.
3. (A) Replace 'very senior' by 'much senior'. 'Very' is used with positive degree adjectives, 'much' is used with comparative degree adjectives.
4. (C) Replace 'hardly hit' by 'hit hard'.
5. (A) Write 'Hardly does she'. Inversion will be used here.
6. (A) Write 'only' before 'with' and not in the beginning of sentence.
7. (B) Replace 'too much' by 'much too'. 'Much too' is used before an adjective and 'too much' is used before a noun.
8. (B) Replace 'know to make' by 'know how to make'.
9. (C) Replace 'so Asha is ' by 'so is Asha'. Inversion is applied here.
10. (E) No error.

Exercise 21

1. (B) Write how 'skilfully'. 'Skilful' is an adjective, can't qualify a verb.
2. (A) Delete 'almost'. Use of adverb before 'quite' is incorrect.
3. (B) Write 'to be kind enough'. Adverb 'enough' is used after the word it qualifies.
4. (D) Replace 'still' by 'yet', 'yet' is generally used in negative sentence while 'still' is used in affirmative sentence.
5. (A) Replace 'surely' by 'sure'.
6. (D) Replace 'fairly' by 'rather'.
7. (A) Write 'he earns only'. 'Only' should be used before the word it qualifies.
8. (B) Replace 'where' by 'when'.
9. (A) Delete 'else', it is superfluous here.
10. (E) No error.
11. (B) Write 'and so he always tries to'.

Exercise 22

1. (C) Replace 'was' by 'were'.
2. (A) Replace 'saves' by 'save'.
3. (A) Replace 'was' by 'were'.
4. (C) Replace 'are' by 'is'. Subject 'merit' is singular.
5. (D) Replace 'are' by 'is'. The subject 'condition' is singular.
6. (C) Replace 'are' by 'is'. The subject 'smell' is singular.
7. (D) Replace 'speaks' by 'speak'. The subject is 'The condolence messages' which is plural.
8. (C) Replace 'have' by 'has'. Subject 'Economic cooperation' is singular.
9. (B) Replace 'have' by 'has'. 'band' is a collective noun so singular verb is used.
10. (C) Replace 'are' by 'is'. Singular verb is used with 'the number'.

Exercise 23

1. (D) Replace 'has been' by 'have been'. Subject 'manager's comments' is plural.
2. (C) Replace 'was' by 'were'. Subject 'details' is plural.
3. (C) Replace 'passes' by 'pass'. Noun 'writers' is plural.
4. (C) Replace 'is' by 'are'. Noun 'features' is plural.
5. (D) No error.
6. (C) Replace 'have' by 'has'. 'Governing body' is a collective noun, so singular verb will be used.

7. (D) Replace 'their' by 'its'.

8. (B) Replace 'are' by 'is'. 'Five quintals' represents a definite weight and used as collective noun so singular verb will be used.

9. (A) Replace 'have' by 'has'. 'Dickens' is the name of a person.

Exercise 24

1. (D) Write 'are' after hopes. If two different verbs are needed with two nouns, use separate verb with each noun.

2. (A) Write 'be' after 'may'.

3. (B) Say 'richest men'. Remember to use plural noun after 'one of the'.

4. (A) Say 'we can get almost' to make the meaning logical.

5. (C) Replace 'drink' by 'drinks' as singular verb is used in such sentences.

6. (B) Replace 'is' by 'are'. When two nouns are joined with and use plural verb.

7. (B) Say 'men'. See the explanation of question (3).

8. (B) Replace 'were' by 'was'. Magistrate and collector is one person so singular verb should be used.

9. (B) Replace 'are' by 'is'. Horse and carriage represents one unit.

10. (B) Replace 'are' by 'is'. Rice and fish is used as a unit.

Exercise 25

1. (B) Say 'tallest men'.

2. (C) Replace 'that a crime' by 'that committed a crime'.

3. (D) Write 'than it was last year' to make the comparison logical.

4. (A) Say 'I have scarcely'. This is a question of misplacement of an adverb.

5. (C) Write 'brings'.

6. (C) Replace 'are' by 'is'. The verb should agree with the noun that comes first in such constructions.

7. (B) Replace 'are' by 'is'. 'Bread and butter' is used as a unit.

8. (C) Replace 'has' by 'have'. The verb should agree with the nearest noun in such constructions.

9. (A) Say 'There is'. Use singular verb with 'nothing but'.

10. (B) Replace 'is' by 'am'.

Exercise 26

1. (A) Say 'Ganesh and I'. Reflexive pronoun cannot be used as such.

2. (D) Delete 'they'.

3. (A) Change 'Thoroughly' by 'thorough'. Correct the spelling of 'thoroughly'.
4. (C) Place 'on' after 'later'.
5. (A) This is a question of Inversion. Place 'had' after 'hardly' and delete 'as'.
6. (C) Change 'what' by 'that' Relative pronoun 'that' is used after anything, nothing.
7. (B) Change 'for' by 'to' with regard to is a phrase.
8. (B) Use 'a' before 'good'. Here, 'good pre school education' is used as idiomatic phrase.
9. (A) Say 'I had known'. This is a conditional structure.
10. (B) Remove 'was'. Use of 'was' is unwanted.

Exercise 27

1. (C) Change 'do' by 'does', The subject 'The Rajdhani Express' is singular.
2. (D) Change 'till' by 'even'.
3. (B) Delete 'much'. 'Much' is used before adjective of past participle.
   For example: Sheela is much interested in this project.
4. (C) Change 'tomorrow' by 'the next day'.
5. (B) Place 'as' after 'quick'.
6. (E) No error.
7. (D) Change 'paid' by 'paying'.
8. (A) Change 'would have' by 'had'. This is a conditional structure.
9. (C) Change 'are' by 'have been' before 'living'. The sentence is in present perfect continuous tense.
10. (B) Change 'did he prosper' by 'has he prospered'.

Exercise 28

1. (C) Change 'shop' by 'shops'. Use plural form of nouns after any of, most of, one of etc.
2. (B) Change 'where' by 'when'. Use 'when' with 'hardly'.
3. (D) Change 'through' by 'thorough'.
4. (A) Change 'brother' by 'brothers'. See explanation of question no. 1.
5. (E) No error.
6. (B) Change 'have' by 'has'. The subject 'The minister' is singular.
7. (C) Change 'will' by 'should'. Use 'should' after 'lest'.
8. (D) Change 'for' by 'from'. Wrong use of preposition.
9. (C) Change 'employee' by 'employees'.
10. (E) No error.

Exercise 29

1. (D) 'But for little modification' should be changed either by 'but for without modification' or by 'but with a little modification'.
2. (D) Change 'either' by 'neither'.
3. (A) Place 'other' after 'No' to make the construction logical.
4. (D) Place 'a' before 'singer'. 'Singer' is a countable noun.
5. (C) Change 'habit' by 'habits'.
6. (E) No error.
7. (D) Change 'could' by 'can'. The sentence is in present tense.
8. (D) Change 'to' by 'into'. Wrong use of preposition.
9. (E) No error.
10. (D) Change 'have' by 'had'. The sentence is in past tense.

Exercise 30

1. (D) Write 'were' instead of 'was'. The subject 'All the people' is plural.
2. (D) Write 'correctly' instead of 'correct'. 'Correct' is an adjective that can't qualify a verb.
3. (D) Delete 'the' before 'jail'. 'Escape from jail' is an idiomatic phrase.
4. (C) Write 'had' instead of 'was' (set the rules of reported speech).
5. (C) Delete 'than'. Use of 'than' is superfluous.
6. (A) Write 'go' instead of 'went'.
7. (C) Write 'larger' instead of 'largest'. In such constructions, comparative degree should be used in both parts.
8. (D) Write 'for' instead of 'since'. 'For' is used for period of time.
9. (A) Write 'He has built not only'. See the rules of conjunction.
10. (D) Write 'late' instead of 'lately'.

Exercise 31

1. (D) Say 'besides'. 'Beside' means 'side by' while 'besides' means 'in addition to'.
2. (A) Say 'If I had been you'. This is a conditional structure.
3. (C) Say 'was' for 'were'. The subject 'not one' is singular.
4. (B) Write 'children' instead of 'child'.
5. (C) Write 'was' after 'he'. (See the rules of reported speech).
6. (C) Delete 'he'. Use of 'he' is superfluous.

7. (B) Write 'quickly' instead of 'quick'. 'Quick' is an adjective and can't qualify a verb (walked).
8. (D) Delete 'more'. Avoid double comparatives in a sentence.
9. (A) Write 'exercises' instead of 'exercise'. With singular number third person subject (Dinesh), add s or es with the verb.
10. (E) No error.

Exercise 32

1. (E) No error.
2. (D) Write 'to' instead of 'than'. Use preposition 'to' after : prefer, preferable, senior, junior etc.
3. (E) No error.
4. (D) Say 'playing in'.
5. (A) Delete 'to'. Never use 'to' after 'told'.
6. (D) Say 'are for sale'. In such construction, the verb is governed by the noun nearby.
7. (A) Say 'Hindi and Marathi'. Do not use definite article before name of language.
8. (B) Say 'persisted'.The sentence is in past tense.
9. (C) Delete 'not'. We should not use 'not' with until/unless.
10. (B) Change 'such higher' by 'so high' The construction of the sentence is so.... that.

Exercise 33

1. (D) Write 'more' instead of 'much'. 'Much' is not a comparative.
2. (C) Write 'as far as' instead of 'so far as'.
3. (D) Write 'in' instead of 'on'.
4. (B) Delete 'an' and place 'the' before 'attention'.
5. (B) Write 'to go' instead of 'for going'. After 'advise' infinitive is used.
6. (D) Write 'an' instead of 'a' before 'expensive'.
7. (D) Write 'waiting' instead of 'wait'. After 'keep', mind usually 'gerund' is used.
8. (C) Write 'us' instead of 'we'. After preposition, pronoun in objective form is used.
9. (D) Say 'its' for 'their'. The subject 'ruling party' is singular , so singular pronoun will be used.
10. (C) Delete 'to'. Use of 'to' here is unwanted.

Exercise 34

1. (C) Write 'help' instead of 'helps'. Subject 'two people' is plural.
2. (D) Write 'one' instead of 'a'. When numeral adjective 'seven' is used in one part , we should use 'one'.

3. (C) Say 'to take'. Infinitive will be used.
4. (C) Say 'good or bad' or change 'is' to 'are' in part (C).
5. (C) Add 'as' after 'almost'.
6. (A) Say 'it being'. This is a question of dangling participle.
7. (D) Say 'might have'. This is a question of conditional sentence.
8. (C) Say 'of us'.
9. (D) Change 'what' to 'that'.
10. (B) Change 'a' by 'the'. 'Letter' is particularised.

Exercise 35

1. (B) Write 'proclaims' instead of 'proclaim'. When two nouns joined by 'and', have every/each attached with them, singular verb should be used.
2. (C) Write 'John's' instead of 'John'. The comparison should be logical.
3. (C) Say 'a little'. 'Little' means ' almost no', while 'a little' means 'some'.
4. (C) Say 'a little'. 'Little' means 'almost no', while a 'little' means 'some'.
5. (A) Write 'John's' instead of 'John'.
6. (A) Write 'are' instead of 'is'. The subject 'reasons' is plural.
7. (D) Say 'a right'.
8. (D) Say 'will he?' Learn the rules of question tag.
9. (A) Change 'not only satisfies' by 'satisfies not only'. Same part of speech must be used after 'not only.... but also'.
10. (D) Delete 'do not'. Use of 'do not' with 'until/unless' should usually be avoided.

Exercise 36

1. (B) Say 'brought out'.
2. (B) Say 'the Greeks'. Use 'the' before nationality words.
3. (A) Write 'whatever may be his intention'.
4. (A) Write 'kinds' instead of 'kind'.
5. (C) Delete 'due to the fact'. Its use with reason is superfluous.
6. (A) Say 'The person'. Here, the person has become particular.
7. (B) Say 'the only'.
8. (B) Say 'recommend'. The subject is plural.
9. (E) 'No error'
10. (C) Say 'do not hold water'.

Exercise 37

1. (D) Place 'are' after 'you'. 'You' is such a pronoun that have same form in nominative and objective case. See the following sentences:
   I like her more than (I like) you.
   I like her more than you (like her)
   To make the sense clear, it is necessary to place 'are' after you.
2. (C) Write 'banks' instead of 'bank'.
3. (A) Write 'whom' instead of 'who'.
4. (E) No error.
5. (B) Write 'rays' instead of 'ray'.
6. (C) Delete 'till'. The use of 'till' is superfluous.
7. (C) Write 'those' instead of 'that'.
8. (C) Write 'takes' instead of 'take'.
9. (E) No error.
10. (A) Say 'It being'. This is a question of dangling participle.

Exercise 38

1. (C) This is a passive sentence. Change 'to lower down' by 'should be lowered down'.
2. (A) Either use only 'Despite' or 'inspite of'. We must not use 'of' after 'despite'.
3. (B) Remove 'which'.
4. (B) Delete 'himself'. Use of emphatic pronoun 'himself' is unwanted here.
5. (D) Say 'their'. Subject 'The Prime Minister and the Union Home Minister' is plural so plural pronoun will be used.
6. (D). Delete 'he'. Use of 'he' is unwanted.
7. (D) Say 'him' for 'them'. The subject 'teacher' is singular.
8. (E) No error.
9. (B) Write 'one's' instead of 'his'. 'One's' is the possessive pronoun of 'one'.
10. (E) No error.

Exercise 39

1. (B) Use 'fairly' instead of 'rather'. 'Rather ' is used in negative or bad sense, while 'fairly' is used in positive sense.
2. (C) Use 'had' instead of 'has'. The whole sentence is in the past tense.
3. (C) Say 'in a bad mood'.
4. (A) Say 'an almirah'. Use indefinite article before countables. 'An' is used with words pronounced with vowel sound.

5. (B) Say 'the meek and the humble'.
6. (E) 'No error'
7. (B) Replace 'decide' by 'decides' or ' decided'.
8. (C) Replace 'geater' by 'greatest'.
9. (A) Say 'accused of'. Wrong use of preposition.
10. (E) 'No error'.

Exercise 40

1. (D) Say 'few'. 'Few' means 'almost no'.
2. (D) Say 'a singer and scientist'. When two nouns represent one person, use article before the first noun.
3. (D) Replace 'has' by 'had'. The sentence is in the past tense.
4. (D) Write ' apply' before 'brake'.
5. (A) Write 'a' before 'rainy day'. Use article ' a/an' before countables.
6. (E) No error.
7. (B) Say 'the famous'
8. (D) Say 'before the investigating committee'
9. (D) Replace 'until he does not try' by 'till he tries'. Do not use negative (does not) with 'until'.
10. (B) Replace 'has' by 'have' . The subject 'those great sons' is plural.

Exercise 41

1. (A) Replace 'passes' by 'pass' as subject 'they' is plural.
2. (B) Say 'quarrel over'. Wrong use of preposition.
3. (D) Say 'no sense in going'. Gerund should be used instead of infinitive here.
4. (D) Delete 'on' after 'affects'. The use of 'on' is unwarranted here.
5. (B) Say 'with him'. Wrong use of preposition.
6. (D) Replace 'played' by 'playing'.
7. (B) Write 'at' after 'firing'.
8. (A) Replace 'telling' by 'tell'.
9. (D) Replace 'going' by 'goes'.
10. (C) The part should be written as 'he would certainly be'.

Exercise 42

1. (A) Say 'the teacher of Mathematics'.
2. (B) Replace 'clear' by 'clearly'. 'Clear' is an adjective so can't qualify a verb.
3. (B) Replace 'rudely' by 'rude'. 'Rudely' is an adverb, can't qualify a noun as such.

4. (D) Replace 'hit' by 'hitting'. Use gerund after preposition (from).
5. (B) Replace 'worst' by 'worse'. Comparative degree is used for comparing two things.
6. (D) Say 'for the last four years'. 'For' is used for period of time .
7. (B) Say 'to' for 'in'.Wrong use of preposition.
8. (A) Say 'was going on'.
9. (D) Say 'ill of others'.
10. (E) No error.

Exercise 43

1. (A) The part should be written as 'Monisha was about to'.
2. (D) Replace 'are' by 'were'. The sentence shows action in the past tense.
3. (E) No error.
4. (C) Say 'loudly'. 'Loud' is an adjective so cannot qualify a verb.
5. (A) Replace 'fastly' by 'fast'.
6. (C) Replace ' nice' by 'nicely'.
7. (B) Repalce 'best' by 'better' as comparative degree is used for comparing two things.
8. (B) Replace 'rescue' by 'rescuing'. Use gerund after preposition (in).
9. (E) No error.
10. (D) Say 'the greater'. Use 'the' before both the comparative degrees in such sentences.

Exercise 44

1. (D) Remove 'most'. 'Unique' and 'most' both have superlative effect, only one should be used.
2. (C) Delete 'much'. Use of 'much' after 'too' is superfluous.
3. (C) Replace 'run' by 'running'.
4. (B) Write 'as' before 'to'. The sentence structure is based on so.... as construction.
5. (D) Say 'more expensive'. Or 'the less costly'.
6. (B) Say 'to accept willingly and cheerfully'
7. (A) Add 'they' before 'being'. This is a question of dangling participle.
8. (A) Say 'first'.
9. (B) Say 'the best soldier'. Use 'the' before superlative.
10. (D) Say 'from beginning to end'. 'Beginning to end' is an idiomatic phrase.

Exercise 45

1. (D) Say 'very fast'.
2. (A) Say 'how carefully'.
3. (D) Say 'the least arrogant'.
4. (C) Replace 'its' by 'their'.
5. (B) Omit 'due to the fact'. When we have used reason in part (A), the use of 'due to the fact' become superfluous.
6. (C) Write 'had' before 'adopted'. The construction of the sentence is conditional.
7. (A) Say 'with a little patience'. Little means 'no', have negative effect.
8. (A) Replace 'brother in laws' by 'brothers in law'. When pluralising a compound noun, remember to pluralise the root word.

   daughter in law — daughters in law.

   step daughter — step daughters.
9. (C) Replace 'with' by 'to'.
10. (C) Replace 'too much' by 'much too'. 'Too much + noun' and 'much too + adjective' are correct constructions. For example: Too much difficulty, much too difficult.

Exercise 46

1. (C) Replace 'but' by 'than'. 'than' will be used after 'other'.
2. (A) Replace 'Good night' by 'Good evening'. Good night is used at the time of final departure.
3. (B) Replace 'vegetable' by 'vegetables'. Vegetable is countable here.
4. (B) Remove 'more'. Avoid using double comparatives as such.
5. (E) No error.
6. (D) Say 'more intelligent'. For comparison between two, use comparative degree.
7. (D) Say 'had never been'.
8. (C) Say 'hard won freedom'. 'Hardly' has a negative effect, means 'no'.
9. (B) Change 'heavy' to 'heavily'.
10. (B) Say 'very neatly and carefully'. Neat and careful are adjectives so can't qualify a verb.

Exercise 47

1. (A) Say 'from his attitude'.
2. (B) Say 'amount of radiation'.
3. (D) Say 'a new one'. Here 'one' is a pronoun.

4. (B) Say 'goes abroad'. 'Goes abroad' is a phrase.

5. (D) Say 'aversion to'. Wrong use of preposition.

6. (B) Say 'call in question'. It is a phrase.

7. (B) Say 'usher in'. Use preposition, where necessary.

8. (C) Say 'spark off'. Use preposition, where necessary.

9. (C) Write 'people' after 'good', good and bad people means people who are good as well as bad. A red and white shirt means 'A shirt which is red and white shirt'. A red shirt and a white shirt- menas two shirts - one red and other white.

10. (B) Replace 'were' by 'was'. After 'two thirds', if the noun is singular, verbs will also be singular.

Exercise 48

1. (B) Replace 'you will ask' by 'you ask'. In such sentences, we should use present indefinite after : if, until, as well as, after, when etc.

2. (C) Replace 'from leaving' by 'to leave'. After 'forbid', infinitive should be used. For example: She forbade me to go there.

3. (A) The part should be written as 'you must tell me either'.

4. (D) No error.

5. (C) Replace 'must' by 'should'. In a sentence, use of both 'necessary' and 'must' is wrong.

6. (B) Write 'one' before 'hundred'.

7. (C) Replace 'against' by 'to'. After prejudicial, use preposition 'to'.

8. (A) Replace 'am hearing' by 'hear'.

9. (B) Replace 'informations' by 'information'. Information is uncountable, we can't pluralise it by adding s.

10. (B) Replace 'to do' by 'in doing'. Persist takes 'in' preposition.

Exercise 49

1. (B) Replace 'is costing' by 'costs'.

2. (B) Replace 'how am I' by 'how I am'. The sentence is not interrogative. It is assertive.

3. (C) Say 'a perceptible change'.

4. (E) No error.

5. (B) Say 'go to bed'. We should not use 'the' with bed when the purpose is to sleep. See rules of article.

6. (B) Delete 'suppose' or 'if'. Using 'if' with 'suppose' is superfluous.

7. (D) Say 'very good'. 'Too' has negative effect here.

8. (E) No Error.

9. (B) Say 'his joining', to make the meaning of the sentence clear.

10. (C) Use of sanctum is superflous.

Exercise 50

1. (B) Replace 'on' by 'in'.

2. (C) Replace 'catches' by 'caught'. The sentence is in past tense.

3. (B) Write 'from his uncle a telegram'. The relative pronoun (which) should be placed near the antecedent(telegram).

4. (B) Replace 'suits' by 'suited'. The use of 'yesterday' shows that the action took place in past.

5. (D) Replace 'more' by 'many' or ' some more'. Ram Lal bought more shares of that company than Shyam Lal. It is correct, because here 'more' is used for comparison.

6. (A) Replace 'simplest solution' by 'A simpler solution'.

7. (D) Add 'to learn'. Now the meaning of the sentence is clear.

8. (C) Replace 'are' by 'is'. Subject 'The only good thing' is singular.

9. (B) Say 'lamenting for'.

10. (B) Say 'material'.

Exercise 51

1. (C) Write 'who'for 'whom'.

2. (B) Say 'would teach'.

3. (D) Say 'enjoyed himself'. Reflexive pronoun will be used here.

4. (B) Replace 'with' by 'on' or 'over'. Wrong use of preposition.

5. (A) Write 'has' before 'left'.

6. (D) Replace 'bad' by 'badly'. 'bad' is an adjective and can't qualify an adverb (very).

7. (A) Replace 'would have' by 'had'. The construction of the sentence is based on =
If + had + v-3 ..... would have + v-3

8. (D) Replace 'do' by 'did'. The sentence is in past tense.

9. (D) Replace 'evidences' by 'witnesses'.

10. (A) Place 'not only' after eminent instead before. Learn the rules of correlative conjunctions.

Exercise 52

1. (D) Replace 'opening' by 'open'.
2. (B) Replace 'since' by 'for'. 'for' is used for period of time, and 'since' for point of time.
3. (C) Replace 'shall' by 'would'. The sentence is in past tense.
4. (B) Say 'whom'.
5. (A) Add 'he' before 'destitute'. This is a question of dangling participle.
6. (E) No error.
7. (D) Say 'they/these' for 'it'.
8. (A) Say 'my being'. Possessive pronoun is used in such constructions.
9. (E) No error.
10. (C) Add 'themselves' after 'adapt'.

Exercise 53

1. (C) Replace 'but' by 'for'.
2. (A) Remove 'have'. The sentence is in past tense.
3. (B) Use 'information' in place of 'informations'. Information can't be pluralised by adding(s).
4. (A) Use 'reason' in place of 'reasons'.
5. (B) Remove 'to'. Wrong use of preposition.
6. (A) Say 'has been running'. When 'since' is used, the sentence should be in perfect tense.
7. (A) Insert 'will' before 'have'.
8. (A) Say 'gratitude'.
9. (C) Remove 'that', use of that is unwanted.
10. (A) Remove 'off'.

Exercise 54

1. (C) Delete 'of'. Do not use 'of' after 'comprise'.
2. (B) Delete 'among'. Here use of 'among' is superfluous.
3. (C) Use 'are' instead of 'is'. Subject is plural.
4. (C) Say 'wondering' for 'to wonder'.
5. (A) Say 'had we'. This is a question of inversion.
6. (B) Say 'had looked. With past tense, we cannot use present.
7. (C) Use 'would have taken'. This is a question of conditional sentence.
8. (B) Say 'much' for 'very'. 'Much' is usually used with past participle.
9. (C) Say 'reach'.
10. (B) Use 'lay' for 'lied'. 'Lay' is the past of 'lie'.

Exercise 55

1. (C) Say 'and cannot be found out'.
2. (B) Say 'differently'.
3. (C) Say 'the blind'. 'The blind' itself refers blind people.
4. (A) Say 'took to drinking'.
5. (C) Say 'a lot of money'.
6. (A) Say 'broadcast'. 'Broadcast' is the past participle of 'broadcast'.
7. (A) Say 'so many cattle'. We cannot use 'much' for countables.
8. (D) No error.
9. (D) No error.
10. (C) Use 'and' for 'as well as'. The construction of the sentence suggests the use of conjunction both....and.

Exercise 56

1. (A) Use 'been' after 'has', to make the meaning of the sentence clear.
2. (B) Say 'so that' for 'so'. 'So that' will be used to make the meaning clear.
3. (C) Say 'that the defeat'.
4. (D) No error.
5. (D) No error.
6. (C) Use 'me' for 'I'. Objective form of pronoun will be used.
7. (C) Say 'on all hours' for 'in all hours'. Wrong use of idiomatic phrase.
8. (B) Say 'far higher'.
9. (C) Replace 'for' in place of 'since'. 'For' is used for period of time.
10. (B) Say 'into' for 'n'. 'Into' is used for movement like jumped into, leapt into etc.

Exercise 57

1. (C) Say 'the train had left'. This is a sentence of past perfect with two actions taking place.
2. (B) Delete 'the'. Do not use 'the' before name of a subject.
3. (B) Say 'has surrendered'. Singular verb will be used in such construction.
4. (A) Say 'had written'. This is a conditional sentence, use V-III after if + noun/ pronoun.
5. (B) Say 'has been'. The subject 'a debate' is singular.
6. (D) No error.
7. (B) Say 'for revising'. Wrong use of preposition.

8. (C) Delete 'that'. Use of 'that' is unwanted.
9. (B) Delete 'together'. It is superfluous.
10. (D) No error.

Exercise 58

1. (D) No error.
2. (D) No error.
3. (B) Say 'if one is happy'.
4. (A) Add 'done' after 'have'. If different forms of verb are needed with different auxiliaries, use them.
5. (A) Say 'in' for 'at'.
6. (A) Use 'going' for 'go'. 'Ing' form will be used in such constructions.
7. (A) Proper word is 'practises'. Practice is a noun while practise is a verb.
8. (B) Say 'was' for 'were'. The subject is 'whole block of flats', that is singular.
9. (B) Add 'as' after 'much'. The correct combination will be as much as or......
10. (C) Use 'me' for 'I'. Objective pronoun will be used.

Exercise 59

1. (B) Add 'to' after 'not'.
2. (A) Use 'upon' after 'operated'. Use of preposition is necessary.
3. (B) 'Fewer boys'. 'Fewer' is used for countables.
4. (A) Use 'to' for 'with'. Wrong use of preposition.
5. (C) Say 'the falling down of the wall'.
6. (C) Say 'from doing'. Use preposition 'from' after 'prevent'.
7. (B) Say 'than that of Delhi'. Proper comparison must be made.
8. (C) Say 'a hand'.
9. (B) Say 'have' for 'has'.
10. (A) Say 'had we left'. This is a question of inversion.

Exercise 60

1. (C) Use 'with' for 'by'. Wrong use of preposition.
2. (D) No error.
3. (B) Use 'to' for 'at'.
4. (D) No error.
5. (B) Use 'inconsiderate' for 'unconsiderate'.
6. (C) Use 'until' for 'till'.
7. (C) Say 'fell off'. Use of 'from' is wrong.

8. (C) Use 'under' for 'with'. Wrong use of preposition.

9. (D) No error.

10. (B) Say 'let it suffice to say'.

Exercise 61

1. (A) Remove 'of '. Do not use 'of' after 'despite'. It is superfluous.
2. (C) Remove 'was'.
3. (A) Say 'had' for 'as'. The correct expression will be -Hardly had I .....
4. (B) Replace 'such higher' with 'So high'. The sentence is based on the construction so....that.
5. (D) No error.
6. (B) Say 'additions'. Use plural after 'one of ...'
7. (C) Replace 'play' with 'playing' .
8. (A) Place 'better' after 'country' to make the proper comparison.
9. (D) No error.
10. (B) Remove 'a' before 'Colonel'.

Exercise 62

1. (A) Say 'No other student'. While making a comparison, exclusion of the noun being compared is necessary.
2. (B) Say 'is' for 'are'. The subject 'The most important feature' is singular.
3. (D) The sentence is correct.
4. (C) Say 'has' for 'have'. In such construction, the verb is governed ny the noun that comes first.
5. (D) The sentence is correct.
6. (C) Remove 'me'.
7. (A) Place 'not only' after 'we saw'. The parts of speech following correlative conjunctions 'not only ...but also' should be same.
8. (A) Say 'direct'.
9. (A) Remove 'on'.
10. (B) Say 'that' for 'which'. After same, 'that' is used.

Exercise 63

1. (C) 'To' in place of 'for'. Wrong preposition.
2. (A) Remove 'to'. Never use 'to' after 'told'.
3. (C) Use 'for' in place of 'since'. 'For' is used for period of time.
4. (A) Say 'round the clock'.

5. (B) Say 'richest men'. After 'one of ...' use plural noun.
6. (D) No error.
7. (D) No error.
8. (A) Delete 'shall'. After when, if, as soon as etc., don't use 'will' or 'shall'.
9. (A) Use 'has' for 'have'. The subject is singular.
10. (C) Use 'beside' for 'besides'. 'Beside' means side while 'besides' means 'in addition'.

Exercise 64

1. (A) Add 'to' after 'us'.
2. (B) Say 'would leave'. The sentence is in past tense.
3. (A) Delete 'of'. After 'despite' do not use 'of', it is superfluous.
4. (B) Say 'persisted'. The sentence is in past tense.
5. (A) Delete 'the' before 'scholar'. Using article 'the' before both the nouns means that there are two persons.
6. (C) Delete 'more'. Two comparatives should be avoided.
7. (B) Say 'have admitted'. Use of 'been' is unwarranted.
8. (B) Say 'he does not do'. Wrong use of inversion. This is not a question.
9. (D) No error.
10. (B) Say 'each other' for 'one another'. 'Each other' is generally used for 'two'.

Exercise 65

1. (A) Say 'a sense of'.
2. (B) Say 'estimates'. The subject 'Encyclopedia Britannica' is singular.
3. (B) Use 'nor' for 'or'. The sentence is based on conjunction 'neither....nor'.
4. (A) Delete 'shall'. After as soon as/when/as/if, avoid using shall or will.
5. (A) Use 'furniture has'. Furniture cannot be pluralised by adding(s).
6. (A) Delete 'a'.
7. (C) Say 'playing' for 'to play'.
8. (D) No error.
9. (A) Use 'were' for 'was'. Plural verb will be used as the pronoun 'their' suggests plurality.
10. (B) Say 'passed' for 'have passed'.

Exercise 66

1. (B) Delete 'back'. Use of 'back' after 'returned' is superfluous.
2. (A) Say 'break down'.
3. (D) No error.

4. (A) Say 'called off'.
5. (B) Say 'upon' for 'with'.
6. (A) Use 'sully' for 'sullen'.
7. (B) Say 'suggestive' for 'suggestible'.
8. (B) Say 'torrent' for 'torrential'.
9. (C) Say 'to rain'.
10. (D) No error.

Exercise 67

1. (C) Write 'neither' for 'either'.
2. (C) Replace 'beauties' with 'beauty'.
3. (D) No error.
4. (C) Replace 'could' with 'can'.
5. (B) Use 'with' in place of 'for'.Wrong use of preposition.
6. (B) Use 'on' for 'at'.
7. (D) The sentence is correct.
8. (C) Say 'other' for 'another'.
9. (B) Say 'since' for 'from'. With perfect tense, use 'since' or 'for'.
10. (A) Remove 'hardly'. Hardly has a negative effect, don't use two negatives in a sentence.

Exercise 68

1. (A) Change 'began to suspect' by 'suspected'.
2. (A) Delete 'all the more'. Avoid double comparatives in a sentence.
3. (C) Say.... 'would lead them' .... The sentence is in past tense.
4. (B) Write 'and if you had told me all the facts earlier'.
5. (C) Replace 'among' with 'between'. 'Between' is used for two.
6. (B) Delete 'for'.
7. (C) Remove 'more'. 'Preferable' has comparative effect, do not use two comparatives in a sentence.
8. (C) It should be .... 'as it affects the eyes'.
9. (D) No error.
10. (A) It should be .... 'one of our subscribers'. Remember using plural noun after 'one of'.

Exercise 69

1. (C) It should be .... 'has resigned'. Singular verb is used in such construction.
2. (B) It should be .... 'he had been serving'. The use of since shows that perfect tense will be used.
3. (B) It should be .... 'and there was no room for the group of reporters'.
4. (B) Delete 'had'. It should be : 'and spent an enjoyable day'.
5. (A) Replace 'than' with 'but'. It should be : 'It is nothing else but.....'
6. (A) Replace 'are' with 'have'. It should be : 'Now that my children have grown up....'
7. (A) Replace 'in' with 'on'.
8. (D) No error.
9. (B) Replace 'fly' with 'flies'. It should be : 'that flies to the breeding ground'.
10. (D) No error.

Exercise 70

1. (B) Add 'the' before 'Earth'.
2. (A) Say 'Seldom have we been treated'.
3. (A) Delete 'are'.
4. (C) Replace 'among' by 'between'. 'Between' is used for two.
5. (C) Write 'but also miser'.
6. (B) Change 'of the battery' to 'with the battery'.
7. (A) Change 'of' to 'into'.
8. (D) No error.
9. (C) Replace 'an argument rose' with 'an argument began'.
10. (B) Write 'where he has gone'.

Exercise 71

1. (D) No error.
2. (C) Replace 'it' with 'its'.
3. (C) Write 'by bombing at the rail lines and terminals'.
4. (A) Write 'cut off'. Wrong use of preposition.
5. (B) Write 'knock on'. Wrong use of preposition.
6. (C) Write 'hangers on'.
7. (B) Delete 'for'.

8. (B) Change 'from' to 'at'.

9. (B) It should be 'is affecting'. 'Effect' is a noun while 'affect' is a verb.

10. (D) No error.

Exercise 72

1. (B) Replace 'take out' with 'take off '.
2. (A) Replace 'was' with 'were'.
3. (A) It should be-'pretended to be'.
4. (C) It should be-'by the seashore'.
5. (C) It should be-'If I am late'.
6. (D) No error.
7. (A) It should be-'the train was supposed'.
8. (B) It should be-'when she hear'.
9. (D) The sentence does not contain any error.
10. (C) Say 'had been looking'.The context of the sentence shows perfect continuous tense.

Exercise 73

1. (B) Should be 'was broadcast'. The past participle of broadcast is broadcast, not the broadcasted.
2. (B) Should be 'how she could kill the wolf'. It is not an interrogative sentence so no inversion takes place.
3. (A) Should be 'While he was walking slowly in the park'. This is the question of dangling participle.
4. (B) Should be 'travelling has become very pleasant. The use of 'since' shows that the structure of the sentence is in perfect tense.
5. (B) Change 'exposes' to 'expose'. The subject 'The newpapers' is plural.
6. (C) Should be 'and to remember for a longer period of time'.
7. (C) Should be "'we had been looking for a suitable alliance for three years". The sentence is in past tense.
8. (C) Should be "to look after the marketing network of the company".
9. (B) Should be "and the rivers have overflowed their banks". The past participle of 'flow' is 'flowed'.
10. (B) Should be 'show a mind fully alert to'.

Exercise 74

1. (D) Should be 'it was really made in Germany'. The whole sentence is in past tense.
2. (B) Should be 'have no dearth of opportunities to display their art'.
3. (C) Should be 'when the master came'. Use 'when' with 'scarcely'.

4. (B) Should be 'if I had realised'. This is a conditional sentence structure.
5. (A) Should be 'I have been trying to finish'. Perfect structure will be used.
6. (B) Should be 'but he turned it down'.
7. (B) Should be 'against the wall below his window'.
8. (A) Should be 'The foremost criterion of selection we adopted'. 'Criteria' is the plural of 'criterion'.
9. (B) Say 'was' for 'am'.
10. (B) Say 'to' for 'with'.

Exercise 75

1. (A) Should be 'The principle of equal justice'.
2. (D) Should be 'its future programme'.
3. (A) Should be 'Honesty, integrity and intelligence'.
4. (B) Should be 'motorists have to' or 'motorists must'.
5. (C) Should be 'the driver who had met'. 'Who' is used for human beings and 'which' for things.
6. (B) Should be 'has ever sung'. Three forms of 'sing' are; sing-sang-sung.
7. (C) Should be 'could dampen' or 'was able to dampen'.
8. (B) Should be 'any money to pay'.
9. (C) Should be 'were overlooked by'.
10. (D) Should be 'hostilities in that area'.
11. (B) Say 'knock down'.

Exercise 76

1. (A) Replace 'Her'by 'She'. 'Her' is a pronoun in objective case, so can't be used as subject.
2. (B) Replace 'has been' by 'was'. The sentence is in past tense.
3. (B) Replace 'are' by 'is'. Subject 'Duke's collection of early Dutch paintings' is functioning as Collective noun so verb should be singular.
4. (A) Replace 'preferred' by 'prefer'. The sentence is in present tense.
5. (C) Replace 'will bring' by 'brings'.
6. (B) Replace 'told' by 'tell'. In past interrogative, Ist form of verb is used.
7. (B) Replace 'to have spent' by 'to spend'. Use of 'have spent' is illogical.
8. (D) Replace 'want' by 'wants'. With manager (Singular number IIIrd person), 'wants' will be used.
9. (C) Replace 'put it' by 'put them'. Here 'them' is used for books.
10. (D) No error.

Exercise 77

1. (B) Replace 'beside' by 'besides'.
2. (A) Economics is name of a subject so 'is' will be used.
3. (D) Replace 'has gone'by 'went'. The sentence is in past tense.
4. (D) Replace 'the most' by 'more' as 'More' is used for comparison of two.
5. (A) Replace 'wrote' by 'write'.
6. (B) Replace 'worst' by 'worse'. For comparison, use comparative degree.
7. (B) Replace 'are' by 'is'. Noun 'driver' is singular.
8. (A) Replace 'peoples' by 'people'.
9. (C) Replace 'is' by 'was'.
10. (B) Replace 'little of' by 'some of'. 'Little' is used for uncountables.

Exercise 78

1. (D) Replace 'might by 'should'. 'Lest' is always followed by 'should'.
2. (C) Replace 'does not speak' by 'speaks'. 'Unless' is itself negative.
3. (A) Place 'it' before 'Being. This is the problem of unrelated participle.
4. (B) Replace 'who' by 'as' or 'that'. With 'such', 'as' or 'that' is used.
5. (B) Replace 'they' by 'he'. Librarian and cashier refers one person.
6. (B) Delete 'most'. 'Perfect' is itself a superlative.
7. (B) Replace 'which' by 'that'. 'What' is followed by 'that' instead of 'which'.
8. (C) Replace 'were' by 'was'. Statesman and politician refers one person.
9. (B) Delete 'to'.
10. (C) Put 'from' before 'being'. 'Prevented' is followed by preposition 'from'.

Exercise 79

1. (B) Replace 'my child' by 'child's'.
2. (D) Replace 'drink' by 'drinking'.
3. (C) Replace 'any' by 'some'. 'Some' is used in affirmative.
4. (C) Replace 'as to' by 'of'. 'Aware' is followed here by preposition 'of'.
5. (E) No error.
6. (A) Replace 'Crossing the road' by 'When he was crossing the road'. This is the problem of unrelated participle.
7. (C) Replace 'were' by 'was'. Subject of the verb 'captain' is singular.

8. (A) Change 'has come' to 'came'.

9. (B) Replace 'saw' by 'see'.

10. (D) No error.

Exercise 80

1. (B) Replace 'have' by 'has'. 'Many a' is followed by singular verb.
2. (C) Replace 'details' by 'detail'.
3. (B) Replace 'defines' by 'define'. Subject 'authorities' is plural.
4. (D) Replace 'like' by 'as'. 'Such'is usually followed by 'as'.
5. (D) Replace 'of all animals' by 'than any other animal'.
6. (A) Replace 'an essay' by 'the essay'. Here, 'essay' becomes particular.
7. (D) No error.
8. (C) Change 'book' to 'books'. 'One of' is always followed by plural noun.
9. (B) Change 'was' to 'were', as the subject 'Rita and her sister' is plural.
10. (A) Change 'criteria' to 'criterion'. 'Criteria' is plural while, 'criterion' is singular.

Exercise 81

1. (C) Change 'were not' to 'are not'.
2. (B) Change 'all the future problems' to 'the problems of the future'.
3. (A) Change 'forward for' to 'forward to'.
4. (C) Change 'receive' to 'received'.
5. (A) Change to 'We will not only pack'.
6. (C) Avoid using double negative. It should be 'unless full details are given'.
7. (D) Change 'from' to 'to'. Should be 'succumbed to fires recently'.
8. (D) Change 'for' to 'to'. Should be 'and personal attention to each child'.
9. (E) No error.
10. (D) Delete 'independent'. It should be 'way of thinking'.

Exercise 82

1. (A) The word 'physicists' is meaningless.
2. (A) Change to 'No other method of making'.
3. (C) Change to 'in changing the age-old'.
4. (E) No error.
5. (D) Change 'have' to 'has' so that the verb should agree with the subject 'investment'.

6. (D) Change 'his car to start up' to 'his car start up'.

7. (C) Change 'when it catches fire' to 'when it caught fire'.

8. (D) Change 'he went or not' to 'he had gone or not'.

9. (B) Change 'suits him and therefore' to 'suited him therefore'. Superfluous use of 'and'. Incorrect use of tense.

10. (E) No error.

Exercise 83

1. (B) Replace 'six block and thirty flats' by 'six blocks and thirty flats' 'six' is plural so write 'blocks'.

2. (C) Replace 'for better knowledge' by 'for the better knowledge'. 'Knowledge' is particularised in the sentence.

3. (C) Change 'instead of' to 'to'. Preposition 'to' is used with prefer, senior, junior etc.

4. (D) Replace 'by the train' by 'by train'. In phrases like by train , by water, by bus etc., we should not make any change.

5. (C) Replace 'bad habit' by 'bad habits'. After 'one of', noun will be in plural form.

6. (A) Replace 'Myself and Ramanujam' by 'Ramanujam and I'.

7. (B) Change 'puzzled on' to 'puzzled over'. Wrong use of preposition.

8. (B) Change 'inferior than' to 'inferior to'. Wrong use of preposition. Since, inferior, superior, senior, junior, prefer etc. take preposition 'to'instead of 'than'.

9. (B) Change 'complained at' to 'complained about'. Wrong use of preposition.

10. (E) No error.

Exercise 84

1. (A) Delete 'of' after 'comprises'.

2. (A) Change 'Not only the bandits robbed' to 'The bandits not only robbed'. Improper placement of conjunction.

3. (C) Change 'unless she does not have a strong desire to live' to 'unless she has a strong desire to live'. Avoid double negative.

4. (D) No error.

5. (B) Change 'cent per cent' to 'hundred percent'. 'Cent percent' is a wrong expression.

6. (C) Delete 'the' before 'church'. Wrong use of article 'the'.

7. (B) Replace 'talk' by 'talking'.

8. (A) Change 'would have' to 'had'. See the structure of conditional sentence.

9. (B) Change 'peak' to 'peaks'. After 'of', noun is pluralised in such sentences.

10. (C) Change 'student' to 'students'. After 'of', noun is pluralised in such sentences.

Exercise 85

1. (D) Change 'are' to 'is'. When two nouns are joined by the conjunction; 'with', 'as well as', 'together with', 'besides' etc., the verb should agree with the Ist noun.
2. (A) Change 'Men' to 'Man'.
3. (C) Change 'early at' to 'early in'. Wrong use of preposition.
4. (E) No error.
5. (A) Change 'worn' to 'wore'. 'Wore' is the past form of 'wear'.
6. (E) No error. 'None' can be used as singular and as plural also.
7. (D) Change 'from' to 'by'. Wrong use of preposition.
8. (B) Change 'a' to 'an'. Wrong use of article.
9. (A) Change 'love' to 'loved' or 'used to love'. Wrong use of verb tense.
10. (C) Change 'a duty cost' to 'a duty cast'.

Exercise 86

1. (D) Change 'the time' to 'about the time'. Wrong use of preposition.
2. (A) Change 'How do' to 'How did'. Wrong use of tense verb.
3. (B) Change 'sometime' to 'sometimes'. Wrong use of word.
4. (D) Change 'police dog jump' to 'police dog jumping'.
5. (D) Change 'on the door' to 'at the door'. Wrong use of preposition.
6. (C) Change 'of' to 'off'. Wrong use of phrase.
7. (B) Change 'attitudes' to 'attitude'.
8. (B) Change 'from the hand' to 'by the hand'. Wrong use of verb phrase.
9. (D) Change 'for' to 'of'. Wrong use of preposition.
10. (D) Change 'her age' to 'at her age'.

Exercise 87

1. (B) Change 'taller' to 'tallest'. Wrong use of degree of adjective.
2. (C) Change 'who' to 'whom'. Wrong use of pronoun.
3. (C) Change 'or' to 'nor'. Wrong use of conjunction.
4. (C) Change 'since' to 'for'. 'For' is used for period of time.
5. (B) Change 'is divided' to 'are divided'. Here, committee is not used as collective noun.
6. (E) No error.

7. (C) Change 'in its preference on' to 'in its preference to'. Wrong use of preposition.

8. (E) No error.

9. (D) Change 'should like to acquire' to 'would like to acquire'.

10. (A) Change 'If you absent' to 'If you absent yourself'. 'Absent' is used reflexively.

Exercise 88

1. (A) Delete 'The'. Wrong use of definite article 'The'.

2. (C) Change 'are' to 'is'. Wrong use of verb. Here, twenty five kilometers is used as a unit, so singular verb is used.

3. (D) Change 'the French' to 'French'. Do not use definite article 'the' before name of language.

4. (B) Change 'to meet' to 'to meeting'. Wrong use of infinitive.

5. (D) Change 'do you' to 'won't you'. It is a request.

6. (B) Change 'a mason' to 'the mason'. Wrong use of article.

7. (B) Change 'make from' to 'make out'. Wrong use of preposition or phrasal verb.

8. (B) Change 'you will think' to 'will you think'. Proper use of inversion is necessary in questions.

9. (D) No error.

10. (B) Change 'reached there' to 'did we reached there'. Wrong use of inversion.

Exercise 89

1. (A) It should be 'It being a very cold day'. This is the problem of dangling participle.

2. (C) Change 'be' to 'been'.

3. (A) Change 'will insist' to 'insist'. Do not use 'will' after 'if' in such conditional type of sentences.

4. (D) Delete 'had'. It should be 'Subhash Chandra Bose died'.

5. (C) Change 'is' to 'are'. Wrong use of singular verb. When two nouns are joined with the conjunction 'and' use plural verb.

6. (D) Delete 'the' before 'most'. Wrong use of article 'the'.

7. (D) Change 'keep his' to 'keep their'. Pronoun 'their' refer to 'those persons' not 'he'.

8. (E) No error.

9. (B) Change 'are' to 'is'. Wrong use of plural verb with singular subject 'box'.

10. (B) Delete 'to' after 'inform'.

Exercise 90

1. (D) Change 'he does not do it' to 'he did not do it'. Wrong use of tense.
2. (B) Change 'his best' to 'one's best'. Wrong use of pronoun.
3. (A) Change 'deprived from' to 'deprived of'. Wrong use of preposition.
4. (C) Change 'throughly' to 'through'. Unnecessary use of adverb.
5. (B) & (C) It should be : The villager told us 'where the temple was' and even led us to the spot.
6. (D) Change 'than' to 'but'.
7. (E) No error.
8. (C) Change 'to' to 'than'.
9. (B) Change 'manages to play' to 'managed to play'. Wrong use of tense verb.
10. (C) Change 'to reinstated' to 'be reinstated'.

Exercise 91

1. (A) It should be 'Thinking that he had finally found'. The sentence is in past tense so to use present perfect is incorrect.
2. (C) It should be 'telecast by a commercial television channel'. The past of 'telecast' is 'telecast'.
3. (C) It should be 'that you have made a mistake' or 'you have committed a mistake'.
4. (B) It should be 'he has six houses in Mumbai'. Generally, the verb 'have' is not used in continuous form.
5. (B) It should be 'if I was ill'. If the reporting verb is in past , the tense of the reported speech be also past.
6. (C) It should be 'he had bought it'. For the action completed first, use past perfect tense.
7. (B) It should be 'is to reduce matter by an analysis'. Use article a/an before countables.
8. (C) It should be 'it was hardly ten'. Hardly has negative meaning. Avoid using double negative .
9. (C) It should be 'was deceived'. If two nouns are joined with; like , in addition to, together with, etc., the verb will be as per the Ist noun.
10. (C) It should be 'and were seeking a job'. Use past verb before 'seeking'.

Exercise 92

1. (A) Should be: 'As I prefer coffee to tea'. Prefer always takes preposition 'to'.
2. (D) No error.
3. (B) Should be : ".....to find evidence....."

4. (D) No error.

5. (D) No error.

6. (C) Change 'then' to 'than'. 'Than' is used here in conjunctions.

7. (B) Noun 'furniture' can't be pluralised as 'furnitures'. Should be : ".....with all the furniture'.

8. (D) No error.

9. (C) Insert definite article 'the' as. 'The Ganges and the Himalayas'.

10. (B) Change to 'is the better.....'. For the comparison of two, use comparative degree.

Exercise 93

1. (A) Change to 'After he finished the work'.

2. (C) Change 'can' to 'could' as. 'Because they thought that they could now remove it with safety'. The sentence is in past tense.

3. (C) Insert 'the' before United Nations.

4. (B) Change 'was' to 'were'.

5. (B) Should be 'he was addicted to reading the jokes in punch aloud'. Gerund form is used in such sentence structure.

6. (A) Use either first or next in the sentence. Should be, 'Why not stop the first man you meet and ask' Or 'Why not stop the man you meet next and ask'.

7. (C) 'Unique' cannot be compared. Should be, 'a unique development'.

8. (A) 'Put out' means 'to extinguish'. Should be, 'Put out.'

9. (C) Should be, 'on the deck of the ship'.

10. (A) Always use auxiliary 'had' after 'hardly'. Should be, 'Hardly had the rains started'.

Exercise 94

1. (C) Change 'and not found out' to 'and are not found out'. Use of 'verb' is necessary here.

2. (B) Change 'different' to 'differently'. Incorrect use of verb in place of adverb.

3. (C) Change 'leading the blinds' to 'leading the blind'. 'The blind' means 'the blind people'.

4. (A) Change 'took to drink' to 'took to drinking'.

5. (C) Change 'lot of money' to 'a lot of money'as 'A lot of' is a phrase.

6. (A) Change 'broadcasted' to 'broadcast'. 'Broadcasted' is the past of 'broadcast'.

7. (A) Change 'much' to 'many'. 'Much' is used for uncountables.

8. (A) Change 'What, could have provoked him' to 'What provoked him'. Incorrect use of perfect tense.

9. (A) Change 'They were rich zamindars in the thirties' to 'They had been rich zamindars in thirties'.

10. (C) Change 'as well as' to 'and'. Incorrect use of conjunction 'as well as'.

Exercise 95

1. (B) Change 'broadcasted' to 'broadcast'.

2. (B) Change 'how could she kill' to 'how she could kill'. Incorrect use of inversion in indirect speech.

3. (A) Change 'While walking slowly in the park'. to 'While he was walking slowly in the park'. This is a problem of unrelated participle.

4. (B) Change 'travelling became very pleasant'. to 'travelling has become very pleasant'. Incorrect use of tense.

5. (B) Change 'exposes' to 'expose'. Incorrect use of singular verb.

6. (C) Change 'and to have remembered for' to 'and to remember for'. Incorrect use of perfect tense.

7. (C) Change 'we have been looking for' to 'we had been looking for'. Incorrect use of tense.

8. (C) Change 'look up the marketing' to 'look after the marketing'. Incorrect use of phrasal verb.

9. (B) Change 'have overflown' to 'have overflowed'. Part (B) should be 'and the rivers have overflowed their banks'.

10. (B) Change 'persist' to 'persisted'. The sentence structure is in past tense.

Exercise 96

1. (C) Change 'was' to 'had'. Incorrect use of tense.

2. (A) Change 'to keep maintaining' to 'to maintaining'.

3. (A) Change 'Being the second' to 'It being the second'. It is a problem of unrelated participle.

4. (D) No error.

5. (A) Change 'Such of those who have not paid the fees' to 'They who have not paid the fees'.

6. (C) Insert 'himself' after 'avail'. 'Avail' is used reflexively.

7. (B) Change 'for' to 'of' ".... of their health..."

8. (C) Omit 'about'. Should be : "....anything left to discuss."

9. (B) Change pronoun 'you' to 'he'. Should be : "..... where he was."

10. (C) Should be : "...... till you finish your work." In such type of sentences, don't use will after; when, as soon as, till, after, as etc.

Exercise 97

1. (A) Replace 'swam by 'swum'. Third form of 'swim' is swum.
2. (B) Delete 'more'. Avoid using double compartives in a sentence.
3. (D) Replace 'A' by 'The'. ' With the naked eyes' is correct expression .
4. (A) Replace 'advices' by 'advice'.'advice' is an uncountable noun. We cannot pluralise 'advice' as such (Advices).
5. (B) Delete 'have' after 'they'. This is a conditional sentence with following structure. Had they invited me, I would have attended the function.
6. (B) Replace 'is' by 'was'. Reporting verb is in past so the reported speech will also be in past.
7. (A) Replace 'don't' by 'does not'.
8. (B) Replace 'are' by 'was'. The sentence structure is in Past tense.
9. (A) Replace 'Cattles' by 'Cattle'. 'Cattle' is itself in plural.
10. (B) Replace 'than' by 'to'. Superior, senior, junior, inferior, prior etc., takes preposition 'to'.

Exercise 98

1. (C) Delete 'not'. Avoid double negative.
2. (C) Place 'how' before 'to'.
   For example:
   (i) I do not know how to swim.
   (ii) I don't know how to play carrom.
   (iii) I do not know where to go.
3. (B) Delete 'more'. Double comparatives should be avoided.
4. (D) No Error.
5. (D) Replace 'good' by 'well'.
6. (C) Replace 'as well as' by 'and'. The structure of the sentence is Both ..... and.
7. (B) Delete 'to' after 'resembles'.
8. (A) Replace 'the two first'by 'the first two'.
9. (C) Replace 'country' by 'countries'. After 'one of' and 'most of', use noun in plural form.
10. (C) Replace 'then'by 'when'. 'Hardly', 'Scarcely' takes conjunction 'when'. For example: Hardly/scarcely had she left the hotel when it began to rain.

Exercise 99

1. (B) Replace 'he wrote'by 'he had written'.
2. (D) The correct expression is 'one's' living.
3. (A) Use of 'to' is superfluous.
4. (A) Use of 'do not' is wrong. 'Unless' is itself negative.
5. (B) Place 'had' before 'read'.
   For example:
   (i) After he had reached the station, the train arrived.
   (ii) The patient had died before the doctor reached here.
6. (C) Use of 'other'is superfluous.
7. (C) Replace 'has'by 'have'. Subject 'The issues'is plural.
8. (D) Replace 'its' by 'a'. 'for a picnic' is correct phrase.
9. (B) Replace 'snowed'by 'snows'. The use of future and past like this is an incorrect combination.
10. (A) Replace 'between' by 'among'. 'Between' is used for two and 'among' for more than two.

Exercise 100

1. (A) Replace 'swam' by 'swum'.
2. (B) Delete 'more'. Avoid using double comparatives in a sentence.
3. (D) Replace 'their' by 'his'. With 'everyone, everybody, anyone, anybody', always use singular possessive pronoun (his or her).
4. (B) Replace 'on' by 'of'.
5. (C) Replace 'hung' by 'hanged'. Verb 'hang' has two forms and two meanings as per the following :

	Ist form	IInd form	IIIrd form
(i)	Hang	hung	hung
(ii)	Hang	hanged	hanged

6. (B) Change 'will' to 'would'.
7. (B) Use 'from' after refrain instead of 'with'.
8. (C) Place 'that of' after 'to'.
9. (A) Replace 'none' by 'neither'.
10. (B) Replace 'where had I' by 'where I had'. In 'Indirect narration', the sentence changes from interrogative to assertive.

Exercise 101

1. (B) Replace 'homes' by 'home'. 'At home' is a phrase.
2. (E) No error.
3. (B) Replace 'a' by 'the'.
4. (A) Replace 'is' by 'was'. The whole sentence reflects action in the past.
5. (A) Place 'It' before 'being'. This is the problem of unrelated participle.
6. (B) Replace 'have' by 'has'.

   For example:

   (i) Many a pen is on the stool.

   (ii) Many a person comes here daily.
7. (B) 'Is' will be used after 'a digital computer'. This is an assertive sentence, not an interrogative one.

   See the following examples :

   (i) I do not know where he lives.

   (ii) I know what he says.
8. (C) Replace 'you'll pay' by 'you pay'.
9. (C) Replace 'purchase' by 'purchased'. This is a conditional sentence with the following structure : **Had + Sub + V-III .... + would have + V-III**
10. (E) No error.

Exercise 102

1. (B) Replace 'will' by 'would'. When the sentence reflects an action in the past, it is incorrect to use 'will'.
2. (B) 'From' is superfluous.
3. (A) Delete 'to' before 'help'.
4. (B) Replace 'has' by 'had'.
5. (A) Replace 'need' by 'needs'. Subject 'our country' is singular.
6. (A) Replace 'Instead of' by 'In spite of'.
7. (B) Replace 'for' by 'to'.
8. (D) Replace 'than' by 'to'. Remember to use 'to' after; 'senior, junior, prefer, prior' instead of 'than'.
9. (B) Replace 'last' by 'latter'.

   For example:

   (i) Ramesh and Surersh are friends. The latter is an engineer.

   (ii) Ramesh, Suresh and Megha are friends. The last is a banker.
10. (B) Place 'were' before 'surprised'. This is a passive structure.

Exercise 103

1. (C) Place 'the' before 'eastern'.
2. (B) Replace 'who do I want' by 'whom I wanted'. In indirect narration, the sentence is changed to assertive.
3. (C) Replace 'with' by 'to'.
4. (B) Replace 'will' by 'would'. The tense of the reported speech changes accordingly.
5. (B) Replace 'are' by 'am'.
6. (C) Replace 'than' by 'to'.
7. (E) No error.
8. (C) Use of 'then' is superfluous.
9. (E) No error.
10. (D) Place 'other' after 'any'.

Exercise 104

1. (A) Replace 'Being' by 'That, Because, Since, or As'. In this question, 'Being' is used in place of 'That or Because or Since or As'.
2. (B) Replace 'their' by 'its'.
3. (D) Replace 'A' by 'The'. 'With the naked eyes' is correct expression.
4. (A) Replace 'advices' by 'advice'. 'Advice'is uncountable. We cannot pluralise 'advice' as such (Advices).
5. (A) Place 'It' before 'being'. This is the problem of unrelated participle.
6. (B) Replace 'have' by 'has'. 'Many a' takes singular noun and singular verb.

   For example:
   (i) Many a pen is on the stool.
   (ii) Many a person comes here daily.
7. (E) No error.
8. (E) No error.
9. (A) Place 'had' after 'No sooner'. This is the question of inversion.
10. (A) Use of 'away' after 'fled' is superfluous. This is the question of superfluous expression.

Exercise 105

1. (B) Replace 'is having' by 'has'.
2. (C) Replace 'as' by 'that'. Structure is 'so....that'

   For example:

   (i) He is so poor that he cannot buy a pen.

   (ii) She is so weak that she cannot climb up the stairs.
3. (C) Replace 'Governor chamber' by "Governor's chamber". This is the question of use of apostrophe.
4. (C) Replace 'has' by 'have'. Subject 'Congress dissidents and a wide range' is plural. If the subject is in plural, verb is also in plural.
5. (A) Replace 'would have' by 'had'. This is a conditional sentence with specific structure : **If + Subject + had + V-III + Would have + V-III.**
6. (D) Replace 'were' by 'was'. If the subject is singular, verb is singular. If subject is plural, verb is plural.
7. (C) Place 'other' after 'No'. While making comparison, the item (being compared) is required to be excluded. As : no other girl of this class is so/as beautiful as Rani.
8. (C) Replace 'have' by 'had'. Reporting verb is in past tense.
9. (C) Replace 'have' by 'has'. Subject 'A letter' is singular.
10. (B) Place 'a' before 'kilogram'. 'Kilogram' is a countable noun.

Exercise 106

1. (A) Replace 'is' by 'was'. The sentence reflects an action in the past.
2. (A) Replace 'his' by 'one's'.
3. (A) Replace 'under' by 'in'. For example: Sit in the shade of a tree. Sit under a tree.
4. (C) Replace 'was' by 'is'.
5. (B) Replace 'for' by 'to'.
6. (D) Replace 'than' by 'to'. After, senior, junior, prefer, prior etc., always use 'to' instead of 'than'.
7. (A) Replace 'cattles' by 'cattle'.
8. (B) Replace 'than' by 'to'.

Phrase Substitution (Sentence Improvement)

In questions relating to phrase substitution, a sentence is given with a part of it made bold. This part contains some error. The candidate is required to substitute this part from the phrases given as options in the answer. Select the phrase that best substitutes the bold part of the sentence, thereby making the sentence grammatically correct. If you find no error in the bold part of the sentence, mark your answer as (e).

How to Solve Such Questions?

In most of the competitive examinations, you will find five or ten questions relating to phrase substitution. In such questions, a sentence is given in which a part of the sentence is incorrect, such incorrect part is to be replaced by the other phrase or part, out of the choices given so that the given sentence becomes grammatically correct. In such questions, there is either some grammatical error or wrong use of verbs in the phrase or some other kind of error. Such error is to be detected and replaced with the correct option.

Remember that there is no 'shortcut' of attempting these questions correctly. Learn the grammar rules and their usage . Rules of various grammatical concepts, notions, including conditional sentences, phrasal verbs, idiomatic expressions, prepositions, conjunctions and their proper usage will be of much help in scoring good marks in such type of questions.You should also learn about the unenglish and superfluous expressions as well as the rules governing usage of infinitive, gerunds , and participle.You should give particular attention to the various exceptions to the grammatical rules also. The basic point or the main task is to have good command over the various grammatical rules and notions, in order to secure good score in such type of questions.

PRACTICE EXERCISES

Exercise 1

***Directions (Q.1-5)** : Which of the phrases (a), (b), (c) and (d) given below each sentence should replace the phrase printed in bold type to make the sentence grammatically correct ? If the sentence is correct as it is, mark (e) as your answer :*

1. My doctor knew that I would eventually recover and do the kind of work I **would be doing** before.

(a) would have been doing (b) would have done
(c) had been done (d) had been doing
(e) No correction required

2. If you are thinking about investing overseas, **isn't make** sense to find an experienced guide ?

(a) is it not making (b) doesn't it make
(c) does it make (d) is it making
(e) No correction required

3. In addition **to enhanced their reputation** through strategic use of philanthropy, companies are sponsoring social initiatives to open new **markets.**

(a) of enhancing their reputations (b) to having enhance their reputation
(c) to enhancing their reputation (d) to have their reputation enhancing
(e) No correction required

4. Technology **must use to feed** the forces of change.

(a) must be used to feed (b) must have been using to feed
(c) must use having fed (d) must be using to feed
(e) No correction required

5. The **crime has grown rapidly** in Russia since the disintegration of the communist system.

(a) rapid crime has grown (b) crime has grown rapidly
(c) crimes grow rapidly (d) crimes have been rapidly grown
(e) No correction required

Exercise 2

***Directions (Q. 1-5)** : In the following questions, each sentence has an underlined words or phrase followed by four alternatives. You are required to choose the one that best keeps the meaning of the original sentence if it is substituted for the underlined words or phrase :*

1. Veterinarians usually give dogs an anesthetic so that they don't <u>cry out in pain</u>.

(a) gulp (b) flip
(c) yelp (d) purr

2. City taxes are based on an estimate of the value of one's property.

(a) appraisal (b) forecast

(c) diagnosis (d) outline

3. Although buses are scheduled to depart at a certain hour, they are often late.

(a) listed (b) requested

(c) obligated (d) loaded

4. Because light travels faster than sound, lightning appears to go before thunder.

(a) prolong (b) traverse

(c) repel (d) precede

5. When students do not have time to read a novel before class, they read an outline of the plot instead.

(a) an article (b) a synopsis

(c) a critique (d) an essay

Exercise 3

***Directions (Q. 1-5)** : Which of the phrases (a), (b), (c) and (d) given below each sentence should replace the phrase printed in bold type to make the sentence grammatically correct ? If the sentence is correct as it is, mark (e) as the answer :*

1. The performance of our players was rather **worst than I had expected.**

(a) bad as I had expected (b) worse than I had expected

(c) worse than expectation (d) worst than was expected

(e) No correction required

2. It is always better to make people realise the importance of discipline **than to impose them on it.**

(a) impose it with them (b) impose them with it

(c) imposing them on it (d) impose it on them

(e) No correction required

3. The crops are dying, **it must not had rained.**

(a) must had not (b) must not be

(c) must not have (d) must not have been

(e) No correction required

4. They **were all shocked at** his failure in the competition.

(a) were shocked at all (b) had all shocked at

(c) had all shocked by (d) had been all shocked on

(e) No correction required

5. He is too impatient **for tolerating** any delay.
   (a) to tolerate (b) to tolerating
   (c) at tolerating (d) with tolerating
   (e) No correction required

Exercise 4

Directions (Q.1-10) : *Look at the underlined part of each sentence. Below each sentence are given three possible substitutions for the underlined part. If one of them(a), (b), or (c) is better than the underlined part, select that part as your response. If none of the substitution improve the sentence, choose (d) as your response. Thus, a 'No improvement' response will be signified by the letter (d) :*

1. Just before the commencement of the examination, the invigilator advised us from copying or indulging in any other malpractices.
   (a) against (b) upon
   (c) about (d) No improvement
2. The whole country is disappointed over the defeat of the cricket team.
   (a) on (b) above
   (c) by (d) No improvement
3. If he joins the coaching class so late, I am afraid it will be hard for him to catch up with the others.
   (a) speed up (b) join up
   (c) get in line (d) No improvement
4. If a definite cure for cancer is discovered in few years, it is unlikely that it will be a simpler or safer affair than that of diabetes.
   (a) in some few years (b) in the next few years
   (c) after few years (d) No improvement
5. The tourists insured their luggage because they assumed it must be stolen.
   (a) will be (b) was going to be
   (c) might be (d) No improvement
6. By the end of May each year, the agricultural produce, comprising wheat and gram, goes to the market.
   (a) to markets (b) to market
   (c) into a market. (d) No improvement
7. The old man looked with caution before he crossed the busy street.
   (a) cautiously before (b) at cautiously when
   (c) cautiously when (d) No improvement

8. Make haste lest you should not be caught in the storm.

(a) that you should not be (b) you can be

(c) you should be (d) No improvement

9. The contesting candidates agreed to seek a common platform while canvassing for votes.

(a) have (b) share

(c) find (d) No improvement

10. The new bank clerk kicked off a row with a colleague.

(a) out a (b) on to a

(c) up a (d) No improvement

Exercise 5

Directions (Q. 1-10) : *Look at the underlined part of each sentence. Below each sentence are given three possible substitutions for the underlined part. If one of the alternatives (a), (b), or (c) is better than the underlined part, indicate your response accordingly against the corresponding letter (a), (b), or (c). If none of the substitutions improves the sentence, indicate (d) as your response. Thus, a 'No improvement' response will be signified by the letter (d) :*

1. Other countries have eradicated this disease ten years ago.

(a) eradicated (b) had eradicated

(c) did eradicate (d) No improvement

2. We were not the wiser for all his effort to explain the case to us.

(a) none (b) neither

(c) nevertheless (d) No improvement

3. If I stood alone in defence of truth, and the whole world is banded against me and against truth, I would fight them all.

(a) will be banded (b) were banded

(c) banded (d) No improvement

4. During his long discourse, he did not touch that point.

(a) touch upon (b) touch on

(c) touch of (d) No improvement

5. He died in the year 1960 at 11 pm on 14 July.

(a) on 14 July in the year 1960 at 11 pm

(b) in the year 1960 on 14 July at 11 pm

(c) at 11 pm on 14 July in the year 1960

(d) No improvement

6. For all our powers of reason and understanding, we know a little about life's secrets.

(a) a little of life's secrets
(b) little about life's secrets
(c) nothing about life's secrets
(d) No improvement

7. You have come here with a view to insult me.

(a) to insulting me
(b) of insulting me
(c) for insulting me
(d) No improvement

8. This matter admits of no excuse.

(a) admits to
(b) admits for
(c) admits
(d) No improvement

9. He has not and can never be in the good books of his employer because he lacks honesty.

(a) has not and cannot be
(b) has not and can never been
(c) has not been and can never be
(d) No improvement

10. The logic of the Berlin Wall already had been undermined, but when the news came through that the wall itself had been opened I jumped into a car.

(a) had been undermined already
(b) had already been undermined
(c) had been already undermined
(d) No improvement

Exercise 6

Directions (Q.1-7) : *In each of these questions, some part of the sentence or the whole sentence is underlined. Five choices numbered (a), (b), (c), (d) and (e) rephrasing the underlined part follow each sentence. If the original part itself seems better than the alternatives and 'no change' is desired, choose answer (a) and if not, choose one of the other. For each sentence, consider the requirement of standard written English. Your choice should be correct and effective, not awkward or ambiguous. If a choice changes the meaning of the original sentence, do not select it :*

1. If the present trend continues the cost of a good personal computer system even can be as low as Rs 15,000 soon.

(a) No change
(b) even soon can be as low as Rs 15,000
(c) can soon be as low as Rs 15,000
(d) as low as even Rs 15,000 soon can be
(e) as low can soon be even Rs 15,000

2. As the message of the freedom struggle could not be spread over the government controlled radio, it effectively was carried to the masses by the press.

(a) No change.
(b) it was effectively carried to the masses by the press.

(c) by the effective press it was carried to the masses.

(d) it was carried to the effective masses by the press.

(e) to the effective masses it was carried by the press.

3. From a study of University enrolment figures over the past decade, evidence is that women are increasingly opting for professional courses.

(a) No change

(b) the increasingly opting for professional courses by women is evidence

(c) evidently it is increasing the enrolment of women in professional courses.

(d) it is evident that women are increasingly opting for professional courses.

(e) women are increasingly opting for professional courses, that is evident.

4. The new draft legislation seeks to ensure that some of the profits from the commercialisation of bio-diversity goes to the know how actually possessed by local communities.

(a) No change

(b) goes to the actual communities who possess the local know how

(c) actually goes to the communities that possess the know how locally

(d) to the local communities that possess the know how actually

(e) goes to the local communities that actually possess the know how.

5. The rapid fall in birthrate achieved by China over the 1980s is placing a retiring strain on many old workers who must retire now from the workforce.

(a) No change.

(b) places a strain on the old workers as they retire from the workforce.

(c) is placing a strain on the workforce now as many old workers retire.

(d) is placing many old workers on a strain as they must retire from the workforce.

(e) is placing many old workers who must retire as a strain on the workforce.

6. A recently carried out mega-analysis of two decades of published research does not suggest that there should be an association between coffee drinking and coronary ailments.

(a) No change.

(b) suggests that there is no association between coffee drinking and coronary ailments.

(c) suggests for no association between coffee drinking and coronary ailments.

(d) any association between coffee drinking and coronary ailments is not suggests.

(e) shows that coffee drinking should not be suggested to have an association with coronary ailments.

7. In relation to the forthcoming parliamentary election, the EC clarified that as no legislation had been formulated, there was no question of raising the official ceiling on election expenses of candidates.

(a) No change.

(b) raising the ceiling on official election expenses of candidates could not be questioned.

(c) no question had been raised regarding the official ceiling on election expenses of candidates.

(d) the official ceiling on election expenses of candidates should be raised, there is no question.

(e) there was no need to question the official ceiling on election expenses of candidates.

Exercise 7

Directions (1-10)** : Which of the following phrases (a), (b), (c) and (d) given below each sentence should replace the phrase printed in bold type to make the sentence grammatically correct ? If the sentence is correct as it is, mark (e) as the answer :* ***(Bank PO Exam)

1. It is true that there **has been a considerable decline** in rural poverty.

(a) has been considerably declining (b) was considerably a decline

(c) have been considered decline (d) has a considerable decline

(e) No correction required

2. They **have been attending** classes since the term began.

(a) would attend (b) had attended

(c) would be attending (d) should attend

(e) No correction required

3. He considers the new assignment as more challenging than **much of the other** assignments.

(a) none for the other's (b) most of the other

(c) more of the other (d) rest of the other

(e) No correction required

4. Resolutions must **be introducing quickly to repeal** the outdated laws.

(a) be introducing to quick repeal

(b) have to be introduced to quick repealing

(c) be quickly introduced to repeal

(d) be quick introducing to repeal

(e) No correction required

5. The driver **didn't accede at the demand** of the people as he was aware of the risk involved in it.
   (a) was not accede at the demand (b) didn't accede at demanding
   (c) was not acceded by the demand (d) didn't accede to the demand
   (e) No correction required
6. Though his actions **were severe criticism,** he didn't lose his temper.
   (a) were severely criticised (b) had severely criticised
   (c) were at severely criticising (d) had severe criticised
   (e) No correction required
7. Yogic exercises and meditation **seems to be of help** modern men and women deal effectively with anxiety.
   (a) seem to help (b) seems to be helping
   (c) seem to have help (d) seems to help
   (e) No correction required
8. Despite all the complaints against him, we must admit that his behaviour with other **has always courteous.**
   (a) had always courteous (b) have always courteous.
   (c) has always been courteous (d) has always been courteously
   (e) No correction required
9. **Whom did you intend to** offer the job besides the two young boys?
   (a) Who are you intending to (b) Whom do you intended to
   (c) Who do you intend for (d) Whom had you been intended for
   (e) No correction required
10. She always behaves **as if she has not** care at all about my feelings.
   (a) as though she will not (b) as if she doesn't
   (c) as far as she doesn't (d) like if she does not
   (e) No correction required

Exercise 8

Directions (Q. 1-15)** : Look at the underlined part of each sentence. Below each sentence are given three possible substitutions for the underlined part. If one of them (a), (b) or (c) is better than the underlined part, indicate your response against the corresponding letter (a), (b) or (c). If none of the substitutions improves the sentence, indicate (d) as your response. Thus, a ' No improvement' response will be signified by the letter (d) :* ***(CBS 1998)

1. Being given to understand that there is a vacancy of an assistant in the firm, an application was submitted by me.
   (a) an application has been submitted by myself
   (b) an application by me was submitted
   (c) I submitted an application
   (d) No improvement

2. She drives her car at eighty miles each hour.

(a) an hour (b) every hour

(c) hourly (d) No improvement

3. I hope it will not rain when they have started their journey.

(a) they will have started their journey

(b) they will start their journey

(c) they start their journey

(d) No improvement

4. After a six-hour marathon session, the two political parties are united together.

(a) joined. (b) together.

(c) united. (d) No improvement

5. I gave my niece a children's very colourfully illustrated encyclopedia.

(a) a very colourfully illustrated children's encyclopedia

(b) a child's very colourfully illustrated encyclopedia

(c) an illustrated child's very colourful encyclopedia

(d) No improvement

6. Nearly everyone suffers when unemployment rises.

(a) Everyone nearly (b) Nearly all

(c) Nearly each one (d) No improvement

7. If you wrote to me earlier, I would have easily solved your problem.

(a) were writing (b) had written

(c) have written (d) No improvement

8. Can't you never understand what has been said ?

(a) ever understand (b) rather understand

(c) at all understand (d) No improvement

9. The limestone formations suggest that in the distant past, the area was a vast sea filled with creatures that absorb calcium compounds from the water.

(a) absorbs (b) absorbed

(c) had absorbed (d) No improvement

10. He asked me where was my book.

(a) my book was (b) my book is

(c) is my book (d) No improvement

11. Suddenly she became conscious regarding the presence of a stranger in the room.

(a) about (b) of

(c) over (d) No improvement

12. This is the first time in my memory that the river has overflown the banks.

(a) overflew (b) has overflowed

(c) overflowed (d) No improvement

13. What I learned is that freedom is really the result of how you will remove obstacles.

(a) you would remove (b) you can remove

(c) you remove (d) No improvement

14. The workers are waiting for their pay packet since morning.

(a) would be waiting (b) were waiting

(c) have been waiting (d) No improvement

15. Ensure to contact with as many teachers as possible.

(a) contact (b) contact on

(c) contact to (d) No improvement

Exercise 9

Directions (Q. 1-6) : *Look at the bold part of each sentence. Below each sentence are given three possible substitutions for the bold part. If one of them (a), (b) or (c) is better than the bold part, indicate your response on the answer sheet against the corresponding letter (a), (b) or (c). If none of the substitutions improves the sentence, indicate (d) as your response on the answer sheet. Thus, a 'No improvement' response will be signified by the letter (d) :*

(NDA Exam)

1. I can't tackle this problem which with all its complications **have** confused me.

(a) has . (b) had

(c) will have (d) No improvement

2. My friend **would have missed** the train if he had not hurried.

(a) had missed (b) has missed

(c) missed (d) No improvement

3. We have plenty of time, **isn't it** ?

(a) haven't we (b) have we

(c) is it (d) No improvement

4. The criminal as well as his accomplice **was** arrested.

(a) were (b) are being

(c) have been (d) No improvement

5. The world's population will continue to grow **when** the birth rate exceeds the death-rate.

(a) as long as (b) unless

(c) until after (d) No improvement

6. Until he **does not ask for** an apology, I am not going to reinstate him.
   (a) does ask for (b) asked for
   (c) asks for (d) No improvement

Exercise 10

Directions (Q. 1-10) : Which of the following phrases (a), (b), (c) and (d) given below each sentence should replace the phrase printed in bold type to make the sentence grammatically correct ? If the sentence is correct as it is, mark (e) as the answer : ***(Bank PO)***

1. All the members of the club **were assembled to celebrate** the 50th anniversary of the club.
   (a) had assembled to celebrate (b) were assembling to celebrate
   (c) had been assembled for celebrating (d) assembled to celebration
   (e) No correction required

2. **Increased productivity necessary** reflects greater efforts made by the employees.
   (a) Increase in productivity necessary (b) Increased productivity is necessary
   (c) Increase of productivity necessary (d) Increased productivity necessarily
   (e) No correction required

3. The earnest appeal by the staff members that the salaries be subjected to **upward revision were rejected** by the industrialist.
   (a) upwardly revision was rejected (b) upward revision was rejected
   (c) upward revising were rejectable (d) upwardly revision was rejectable
   (e) No correction required.

4. Speculations and **hypothesising are** the most essential and well known aspects of inventions.
   (a) hypothesis has been (b) hypothesising needs
   (c) hypothesis makes (d) hypothesising confronts
   (e) No correction required

5. The **alarming report** of the building collapse made everyone spell bound.
   (a) alarmed report (b) alarmed reporting
   (c) reporting alarm (d) reported alarm
   (e) No correction required

6. Your good gestures **will highly appreciate.**
   (a) will be highly appreciate (b) will be high appreciative
   (c) will be highly appreciated (d) would be high appreciation
   (e) No correction required

7. Yogic exercise **seems to be help** urban population deal effectively with stress.

(a) seems to be helpful | (b) seems to be helped
(c) seems to help | (d) seemed to be of helping
(e) No correction required

8. They **feel very proudly** that their team had won the match.

(a) feel very proudly | (b) felt very pride
(c) feel very pride | (d) felt very proud
(e) No correction required.

9. The pedestrians **must to be** very cautious while crossing the road.

(a) should have to be | (b) must be
(c) should have | (d) are required to be
(e) No correction required

10. I am sure that he has recovered from his illness **and he will accompany** us to the picnic spot.

(a) and that he will accompany | (b) and that he will be accompanied.
(c) but he will accompany | (d) although he will accompany
(e) No correction required

Exercise 11

***Directions (Q. 1-10)** : In these questions, which of the phrases (a), (b), (c) and (d) given below should replace the phrase given in bold in the following sentence to make the sentence grammatically meaningful and correct. If the sentence is correct as it is and no correction is required, mark (e) as the answer :*

(Indian Bank PO)

1. He will be greatly surprised if he **was felicitated** by his staff members.

(a) if he will have felicitated | (b) unless he was felicitated
(c) if he is felicitated | (d) if he would have felicitated
(e) No correction required

2. Did you know when **shall he be leaving** for higher studies to the USA?

(a) should he be left | (b) he would be leaving
(c) he would be left | (d) would he have left
(e) No correction required

3. The labour contractors reported that they **had finished** the work of building the stone wall.

(a) had been finished | (b) was finished
(c) could be finished | (d) has finished
(e) No correction required

4. For want of financial resources, he was **unable to continue** his studies.
(a) unabled to continue
(b) unable to be continued
(c) unable to have continued
(d) unable to continuing
(e) No correction required

5. He complained of **being unjustly treatment.**
(a) of being unjustly treated
(b) for being injustice in treatment
(c) that unjust treatment being given
(d) for being unjustly treatment
(e) No correction required

6. The donation amount was **such that as I was expected** him to donate.
(a) so that as I expected
(b) such that I expected of
(c) such as that I expect
(d) exactly as I had expected
(e) No correction required

7. It is pity that no one in the family **disapproves by his getting up** late.
(a) disapproved by his getting up
(b) disapproves of his getting up
(c) disapproved that he is getting up
(d) disapproved why he got up
(e) No correction required

8. He is less likely to win **unless he practised** rigorously and regularly.
(a) until he practised
(b) unless he practise
(c) unless he practises
(d) unless he does not practise
(e) No correction required

9. Because it was a stormy night, **he dare not to go** out in the dark.
(a) dared not to go
(b) dare not went
(c) dared not to have gone
(d) dare not goes
(e) No correction required

10. **Just when they reach** the station, the train had departed.
(a) Just before they reach
(b) After they just reach
(c) Just when they had reached
(d) Just before they reached
(e) No correction required

SENTENCE IMPROVEMENT

Exercise 12

Directions (Q. 1-15) : *In these questions, look at the underlined part of each sentence. Below the sentence are given three possible substitutions for the underlined part. If any one of substitutions (a), (b), or (c) is better than the underlined part, choose that substitution as your response. If none of the substitutions improves the sentence, choose (d) as your response. Thus, a 'No improvement' response will be signified by the letter (d) :* **(CDS Exam)**

1. The sun was shining such brightly that Leela had to put on her sun-glasses.
   (a) very (b) too
   (c) so (d) No improvement

2. If I were you, I would report the matter at once.
   (a) be (b) am
   (c) was (d) No improvement

3. The document is concerning your health and that of your family.
   (a) concerns with (b) is concerned with
   (c) concerns (d) No improvement

4. The lady laid out a special dinner for her husband on his birthday.
   (a) laid (b) laid up
   (c) laid by (d) No improvement

5. Epidemics are likely to break off in the areas from where flood-water has receded.
   (a) break out (b) break up
   (c) break in (d) No improvement

6. There is no objection to him joining the party.
   (a) on him (b) to his
   (c) upon his (d) No improvement

7. You are too big to go out alone.
   (a) big enough (b) so big
   (c) very big (d) No improvement

8. One of my old friends has invited me for tea in the evening.
   (a) to take tea (b) to tea
   (c) on tea (d) No improvement

9. Hardly had he saddled the horse <u>than</u> the mare broke loose and galloped down the hill.

(a) that (b) when

(c) than (d) No improvement

10. The speaker tried to work <u>up</u> the emotions of his audience.

(a) round (b) off

(c) in (d) No improvement

11. <u>Until</u> the sky is overcast, I take my raincoat with me.

(a) When (b) Even if

(c) Whenever (d) No improvement

12. His discourse <u>about</u> the meteorology was very stimulating.

(a) on (b) of

(c) concerning (d) No improvement

13. Mira <u>told</u> her brother that she had made a mistake

(a) said to (b) pleaded to

(c) admitted to (d) No improvement

14. You don't want a beggar to look happy <u>isn't it</u> ?

(a) aren't you ? (b) do you ?

(c) don't you ? (d) No improvement

15. The instructor told the student to hold the club lightly to keep his eye on the ball <u>but should not</u> use too much force.

(a) and not (b) and not to

(c) still not to (d) No improvement

Exercise 13

Directions (Q. 1-11) : *In these questions, look at the italicized part of each sentence. Below the sentence are given three possible substitutions for the italicized part. If any one of the substitutions (a), (b) or (c) is better than the italicized part, choose that substitution as your response. If none of the substitutions improves the sentence, choose (d) as your response. Thus, a 'No improvement' response will be signified by the letter (d) :*

1. *It is no good to cry* over spilt milk. ***(NDA)***

(a) It is no good crying (b) It is of no good to cry

(c) It is of no good crying (d) No improvement

2. He has been working *off and on* for several years to compile a dictionary. ***(SBI PO)***

(a) on or off (b) on and off

(c) regularly (d) No improvement

3. Rohit assured Sunita that he *would look* at her work while she was on leave. ***(BSRB)***

(a) would overlook (b) would look after

(c) will look (d) No improvement

4. Newton wanted to *know why did the apple fall* to the ground. ***(CBJ)***

(a) know that why did the apple fall (b) know why the apple fell

(c) know that why the apple fell (d) No improvement

5. He was extremely unhappy because of *the inordinately delay*. ***(Bank PO)***

(a) the inordinate delaying (b) the inordinate delay

(c) the inordinately delaying (d) No improvement

6. *There is no more room* for you in this compartment. ***(Section Officer)***

(a) There is no more accommodation (b) There is no more space

(c) There is no more seat (d) No improvement

7. When he arrived to attend the wedding of his brother, he *had been dressed* in dark suit. ***(NDA)***

(a) dressed (b) was dressed

(c) had dressed (d) No improvement

8. I can always *count on him* in times of difficulty. ***(BSRB Patna)***

(a) count at him (b) count on he

(c) count him on (d) No improvement

9. Sunita told me that she would not mind *to stand and eating* the lunch. ***(Income Tax)***

(a) to stand and eat (b) standing and eating

(c) standing and eat (d) No improvement

10. Modern industrialized communities have lost touch with the soil and do not experience that joy which nature gives and the rich glow of health *that which comes from contact* with mother earth. ***(CBJ)***

(a) which comes from contact with.

(b) which comes out from contact with

(c) which flows how from contact with

(d) No improvement

11. He has been receiving no other message than an urgent telegram *asking him to rush his village* immediately. ***(Bank PO)***

(a) asking him rushing at his village (b) asked him to rush his village.

(c) asking him to rush to his village (d) No improvement

Exercise 14

Directions (Q. 1-7) : *In these questions, look at the italicized part of each sentence. Below the sentence are given three possible substitutions for the italicized part. If any one of the substitutions (a), (b) or (c) is better than the italicized part, choose that substitution as your response. If none of the substitutions improves the sentence, choose (d) as your response. Thus, a 'No' 'improvement' response will be signified by the letter (d) :*

1. Each of our *students pay their* tuition fee at the beginning of the month. ***(Astt. Grade)***
   (a) student pay their (b) students pays their
   (c) students pays his (d) No improvement
2. I told him clearly that he *hadn't ought to do* that to me. ***(Bank PO)***
   (a) ought not to have done (b) ought not done
   (c) ought not has done (d) No improvement
3. The fast train *come a halt to before* crossing the bridge. ***(BSRB)***
   (a) came before to a halt
   (b) came to a halt before
   (c) came to halts before a
   (d) No improvement
4. I took the cycle *which he bought yesterday.* ***(Stenographers Exam.)***
   (a) that he bought yesterday
   (b) that he had bought yesterday
   (c) that which he had bought yesterday
   (d) No improvement
5. The practical importance of the role of the industrialist in the establishment of the new order is greater than the *economist and the politician.* ***(Railways)***
   (a) of the economist and politicians
   (b) that of the economists and the politicians
   (c) that of the economist and the politician
   (d) No improvement
6. The poor villagers *have waited* in the bitter cold more than four hours now. ***(IES)***
   (a) has been waiting (b) had waited
   (c) have been waiting (d) No improvement
7. They succeeded *without hardly* making any effort. ***(CBI)***
   (a) hardly without making (b) with hardly making
   (c) without making (d) No improvement

Exercise 15

Directions (Q. 1-6) : *In these questions, look at the italicized part of each sentence. Below the sentence are given three possible substitutions for the italicized part. If any one of the substitutions (a), (b) or (c) is better than the italicized part, choose that substitution as your response. If none of the substitutions improves the sentence, choose (d) as your response. Thus, a 'No improvement' response will be signified by the letter (d) :*

1. He was urgently in need *to get his eye operation.* ***(CBI)***

(a) of an eye operation. (b) for operation on eye.

(c) for eye to be operated. (d) No improvement

2. *By definition, make a map* is to select certain features as relevant and ignore others.

(a) To make a map by definition (b) In making a map, the definition

(c) Map making is defined as (d) No improvement

3. We demonstrated to them how we *were prepared* the artistic patterns. ***(RBI)***

(a) are prepared (b) have prepared

(c) had prepared (d) No improvement

4. Asking me *why was I absent, I was punished by the Headmaster.* ***(CBI)***

(a) why was I absent, was I punished by the Headmaster.

(b) why I was absent, was I punished by the Headmaster.

(c) why I was absent, the Headmaster punished me.

(d) No improvement

5. Do you *remember to meet her* at my house last year ? ***(UDC)***

(a) remember of meeting her (b) remember about meeting her

(c) remember having met her (d) No improvement

6. If you had attended the meeting, you *would have benefitted* a great deal. ***(Stenographers Exam.)***

(a) would benefit (b) could benefit

(c) benefitted (d) No improvement

Exercise 16

Directions (Q. 1-8) : *In these questions, look at the italicized part of each sentence. Below the sentence are given three possible substitutions for the italicized part. If any one of the substitutions (a), (b) or (c) is better than the italicized part, choose that substitution as your response. If none of the substitutions improves the sentence, choose (d) as your response. Thus, a 'No improvement' response will be signified by the letter (d) :*

1. *Although partially destroyed, the experts were able to infer* from what remained that the treasure was buried in the cave. ***(RBI)***

(a) Although partially destroyed, the experts had inferred

(b) Destroyed partially, the experts were able to infer

(c) Although it had been partially destroyed, the experts were able to infer
(d) No improvement

2. The Principal lamented that though a detailed report was submitted to the management a month ago, *no action is being taken* so far. **(Bank PO)**
(a) no action had taken
(b) no action had been taken
(c) any action had been taken
(d) No improvement

3. May I know *who did accompany you* to the bus station ? **(BSRB)**
(a) who accompanied you
(b) must be
(c) whom did you accompany
(d) No improvement

4. *Leaving aside little room for* misinterpretation, the senior politician offered clarification about his role in the past elections. **(Bank PO)**
(a) Leaving less room for
(b) Leaving little room for
(c) Having left less room for
(d) No improvement

5. We should take up the first item, let *us begin this song*. **(UDC)**
(a) this song begin us
(b) us begin with this song
(c) this song begin us
(d) No improvement

6. *Any able bodied man is* eligible for the job. **(NDA)**
(a) Any able bodied men are
(b) Each able bodied man is
(c) Any able bodied men have been
(d) No improvement

7. *I, your brother and you* will be partners in the business. **(NDA)**
(a) I, you and your brother
(b) You, your brother and I
(c) You, I and your brother
(d) No improvement

8. While we would like *that all Indian children* to go to school, we need to ponder why they do not. **(CDS)**
(a) all Indian children
(b) that all the Indian children
(c) if all the children of India
(d) No improvement

Exercise 17

Directions (Q. 1-5) : *In these questions, look at the italicized part of each sentence. Below the sentence are given three possible substitutions for the italicized part. If any one of the substitutions (a), (b) or (c) is better than the italicized part, choose that substitution as your response. If none of the substitutions improves the sentence, choose (d) as your response. Thus, a 'No improvement' response will be signified by the letter (d) :*

1. *I think in my opinion that* all those who claim to be honest are not really so. **(CBI)**
(a) In my opinion
(b) It seems to me
(c) It is my believing
(d) No improvement

2. Will you *lend me few rupees* in this hour of need. ***(Section Officers Exam)***
(a) borrow me a few rupees
(b) lend my any rupees
(c) lend me a few rupees
(d) No improvement

3. Hold *hands of your child* while crossing the road. ***(CBI)***
(a) your child's hands
(b) your child's hand
(c) hand of your child
(d) No improvement

4. *Have you not reached* in time, we would have lost our lives? ***(Bank PO)***
(a) Had you not reach
(b) If you have not reached
(c) Had you not reached
(d) No improvement

5. You must *accustom yourself with* new ideas. ***(NDA)***
(a) accustomed with
(b) accustom to
(c) accustom yourself to
(d) No improvement

Exercise 18

Directions (Q. 1-10)** : In these questions, look at the italicized part of each sentence. Below the sentence are given three possible substitutions for the italicized part. If any one of the substitutions (a), (b) or (c) is better than the italicized part, choose that substitution as your response. If none of the substitutions improves the sentence, choose (d) as your response. Thus, a 'No improvement' response will be signified by the letter (d) :* ***(CDS 2003)

1. The climate of Delhi is somewhat *like Jaipur.*
(a) like Jaipur's
(b) as Jaipur's
(c) as Jaipur
(d) No improvement

2. His brother *never has* and never will be dependable.
(a) never had
(b) never has been
(c) was never being
(d) No improvement

3. If you *would have remembered* to bring the map, we would not have lost our way.
(a) had remembered
(b) were remembering
(c) remembered
(d) No improvement

4. You must *carry on* my order.
(a) carry off
(b) carry out
(c) carry of
(d) No improvement

5. The boat *was drowned.*
(a) was drown
(b) were drowned
(c) was sunk
(d) No improvement

6. Now I must *beg leave of you.*
(a) beg your leave
(b) beg of your leave
(c) beg off your leave
(d) No improvement

7. *When describing* the accident he was in tears.
   (a) In describing (b) When he was describing
   (c) As describing (d) No improvement

8. The two thieves distributed the loot *between themselves.*
   (a) among themselves. (b) amongst themselves.
   (c) with temselves. (d) No improvement

9. *The preservation of peace* is necessary.
   (a) maintenance of peace (b) establishment of peace
   (c) persuasion of peace (d) No improvement

10. The spirit of democracy had *sped into* our way of thinking.
    (a) leaked into (b) permeated
    (c) soaked into (d) No improvement

Exercise 19

Directions (Q. 1-15)** : Look at the underlined part of each sentence. Below each sentence are given three possible substitutions for the underlined part. If one of them, a, b or c is better than the underlined part, indicate your response against the corresponding letter a, b or c. If none of the substitutions improves the sentence, choose (d) as your response. Thus, a 'No improvement' response will be signified by the letter (d). Errors may be in grammar, appropriate word usages or idioms. There may be a necessary word missing or there may be a word which should be removed.* ***(CDS)

1. More he gets more he wants.
   (a) the more he gets, the more (b) the more he gets, more
   (c) more gets, the more (d) No improvement

2. We had a grand party and we enjoyed very much.
   (a) enjoyed very much (b) We enjoyed ourselves very much
   (c) enjoyed much (d) No improvement

3. All this has been done with a view to improve the living conditions of the poor.
   (a) to improving (b) of improving
   (c) for improving (d) No improvement

4. Let's go for a picnic, shouldn't we?
   (a) Won't (b) Shan't
   (c) Shall (d) No improvement

5. If I have the money, I should have bought this house.
   (a) has had (b) would have
   (c) should have (d) No improvement

6. If you are told of a downright lie about goods to induce you to buy them, you may have a remedy.
(a) about a downright lie (b) a downright lie
(c) downright lie (d) No improvement

7. His father forbade him about entering politics.
(a) from (b) on
(c) to (d) No improvement

8. To some extent, every child takes after his father.
(a) upon (b) for
(c) off (d) No improvement

9. The boss said, 'I shall look at the matter'.
(a) about (b) in
(c) into (d) No improvement

10. I did nothing but laughed.
(a) laughing (b) laugh
(c) laughed aloud (d) No improvement

11. The highest recorded speed of shorthand under championship conditions, is 300 words per minute.
(a) in (b) for
(c) with (d) No improvement

12. There were many petty Rajput Kingdoms in India prior than the coming of the Mohammedans.
(a) prior from (b) prior up to
(c) prior to (d) No improvement

13. Until the last twenty eight years, he has been working in various units of this plant.
(a) for (b) since
(c) during (d) No improvement

14. I hope you will be able to steer ahead of the anti- social elements.
(a) steer out (b) steer free
(c) steer clear (d) No improvement

15. Had Alizee been well, she could participate in the competition.
(a) would participate (b) would have participated
(c) will have participated (d) No improvement

Exercise 20

***Directions (Q. 1–15)** : Look at the underlined part of each sentence. Below each sentence are given three possible substitutions for the underlined part. If one of them, a, b or c is better than the underlined part, indicate your response against the corresponding letter a, b or c. If none of the substitutions improves the sentence, indicate (d) as your response. Thus, a 'No improvement' response will be signified by the letter (d).*

1. On 14 July, 1789 an armed mob seized the Bastille, a royal prison in Paris that came to symbolize the oppressive nature of the Bourbon rules.

(a) was come to symbolize (b) has come to symbolize

(c) had come to symbolize (d) No improvement

2. Please turn off the volume of the radio, so that it is not quite so loud.

(a) out (b) down

(c) in (d) No improvement

3. His access to the throne was a turning point in our history.

(a) acquisition (b) acceptance of

(c) accession to (d) No improvement

4. They were then asked to write a short account of what they have seen.

(a) were seen (b) had been seen

(c) had seen (d) No improvement

5. The printing press is one man's cleverest invention.

(a) cleverest inventions (b) clever invention.

(c) cleverer inventions (d) No improvement

6. What are you looking upon in the dark?

(a) over (b) after

(c) for (d) No improvement

7. We all have to adjust ourselves to the new circumstances.

(a) of (b) with

(c) by (d) No improvement

8. He was a tiny man, barely five feet tall, with a spright walk.

(a) spright walk (b) a sprightly walking

(c) a sprightly walk (d) No improvement

9. Kamal as well as Vimal are leaving for England.

(a) is leaving (b) were leaving

(c) have been leaving (d) No improvement

10. I am waiting for you since 9 o'clock this morning.

(a) was waiting (b) waited

(c) have been waiting (d) No improvement

11. I'll clear out this drawer and you can put your things in it.

(a) clear (b) clear up

(c) clear off (d) No improvement

12. Even as a young boy, he has lacked the inclination to go outdoors and play.

(a) lacks (b) was lacking

(c) lacked (d) No improvement

13. You don't know the mechanism of computer properly isn't it?

(a) Haven't you (b) Do you

(c) Don't you (d) No improvement

14. I find difficult to understand why Vikas has remained silent on this matter.

(a) I find very difficult (b) I find it difficult

(c) I find somewhat difficult (d) No improvement

15. Sodium chloride dissolves in water and so is salt.

(a) so also (b) so will

(c) so does (d) No improvement

Exercise 21

Direction (Q. 1–15) : *Look at the underlined part of each sentence. Below each sentence are given three possible substitutions for the underlined part. If one of them (a), (b), (c) is better than the underlined part, indicate your response on the answer sheet against the corresponding letter (a), (b), (c). If none of the substitutions improves the sentence indicate (d) as your response on the answer sheet. Thus, a 'No improvement' response will be signified by the letter (d). Errors may be in grammar, appropriate word usage or idioms. There may be a necessary word missing or there may be a word which should be removed.*

1. The sun was shining such brightly that Leela had to put on her sun- glasses.

(a) very (b) too

(c) so (d) No improvement

2. If I were you, I would report the matter at once.

(a) be (b) am

(c) was (d) No improvement

3. The document is concerning your health and that of your family.

(a) concerns with (b) is concerned with

(c) concerns (d) No improvement

4. The lady laid out a special dinner for her husband on his birthday.

(a) laid (b) laid up

(c) laid by (d) No improvement

5. Epidemics are likely to break off in the areas from where flood water has receded.

(a) break out (b) break up

(c) break in (d) No improvement

6. There is no objection to him joining the party.

(a) on him (b) to his

(c) upon his (d) No improvement

7. You are too big to go out alone.

(a) big enough (b) so big

(c) very big (d) No improvement

8. One of my old friends has invited me for tea in the evening.

(a) to take tea (b) to tea

(c) on tea (d) No improvement

9. Hardly had he saddled the horse then the mare broke loose and galloped down the hill.

(a) that (b) when

(c) than (d) No improvement

10. The speaker tried to work up the emotions of his audience.

(a) round (b) off

(c) in (d) No improvement

11. Until the sky is overcast, I take my raincoat with me.

(a) When (b) Even of

(c) Whenever (d) No improvement

12. His discourse about the meteorologist was very stimulating.

(a) on (b) of

(c) concerning (d) No improvement

13. Mira told her brother that she had made a mistake.

(a) said to (b) pleaded to

(c) admitted to (d) No improvement

14. You don't want a beggar to look happy isn't it ?

(a) Aren't you? (b) Do you?

(c) Don't you? (d) No improvement

15. The instructor told the student to hold the club lightly to keep his eye on the ball but should not use too much force.

(a) and not (b) and not to

(c) still not to (d) No improvement

Exercise 22

***Directions (Q. 1-15)** : Look at the underlined part of each sentence. Below each sentence are given three possible substitutions for the underlined part. If one of them, (a), (b), (c) is better than the underlined part, indicate your response on the answer sheet against the corresponding letter (a), (b), (c). If none of the substitutions improve the sentence, indicate (d) as your response on the answer sheet. Thus, a 'No improvement' response will be signified by the letter (d).*

Errors may be in grammar, appropriate word usage or idioms. There may be a necessary word missing or there may be a word which should be removed.

1. He has been absent since three days.

(a) from three days (b) during three days

(c) for three days (d) No improvement

2. He bought a new house but disposed it off immediately.

(a) disposed immediately (b) disposed off it immediately

(c) disposed of immediately (d) No improvement

3. He could not be able to think logically because of his illness.

(a) cannot be able (b) was not able

(c) can be unable (d) No improvement

4. Measles is dangerous for adults, too!

(a) with (b) in

(c) to (d) No improvement

5. She was the oldest of the two sisters.

(a) elder of the two sisters (b) oldest between the two sisters

(c) older than her sister (d) No improvement

6. The money he has given is not sufficient enough for the job.

(a) much sufficient (b) sufficient

(c) sufficiently enough (d) No improvement

7. The gypsies had left the village a few days ago.

(a) have left (b) would have left

(c) left (d) No improvement

8. I'll write to you after I shall arrive.

(a) after I shall have arrived (b) after I have arrived

(c) after I arrive (d) No improvement

9. I did nothing but cried.

(a) but crying (b) but cry

(c) but to cry (d) No improvement

10. I hate being late, and if I do, I always feel ashamed.

(a) if I were (b) if I did

(c) If I am (d) No improvement

11. No sooner did his feet touched the ground than the intensity of the disaster dawned upon him.

(a) his feet got touched (b) did his feet touch

(c) his feet had touched (d) No improvement

12. He learnt it sitting under the feet of many great teachers :

(a) before the feet (b) on the feet

(c) at the feet (d) No improvement

13. This chair will collapse as soon as any one will sit on it.

(a) sat (b) sits

(c) is sitting (d) No improvement

14. The boy said that he has read the book.

(a) he has already read (b) he wants to read

(c) he had read (d) No improvement

15. The accused denied the charges framed against him.

(a) declined the charges (b) denied charges

(c) refused the charges (d) No improvement

Exercise 23

Directions (Q. 1–15) : *Look at the underlined part of each sentence. Below each sentence are given three possible substitutions for the underlined part. If one of them (a), (b), (c) is better than the underlined part, indicate your response against the corresponding letter (a), (b) or (c). If none of the substitutions improve the sentence, indicate (d) as your response. Thus, a 'No improvement' response will be signified by the letter (d).*

1. No sooner he saw the Police Superintendent than he disappeared.

(a) No sooner did he see (b) No sooner he had seen

(c) As soon as he see (d) No improvement

2. If I were a king, I would have helped my subjects.

(a) did have helped (b) could helped

(c) would helped (d) No improvement

3. The criminal was ordered to be hanged to death.

(a) hung till death (b) hung to death

(c) hanged till death (d) No improvement

4. A bird in hand is better than two in the bush.

(a) two on bush (b) two in bush

(c) two at a bush (d) No improvement

5. Since I am not new to Mumbai, you must not have come to the Railway Station to receive me.

(a) should not have (b) need not have

(c) ought not to have (d) No improvement

6. She prefers coffee to tea.

(a) than (b) over

(c) for (d) No improvement

7. Our Professor is an authority on the subject which he had been teaching since 1966.

(a) has been teaching (b) is teaching

(c) was teaching (d) No improvement

8. It is high time she changes her job.

(a) must change (b) had changed

(c) changed (d) No improvement

9. I am considering to set up a cyber cafe.

(a) setting (b) set up

(c) setting up (d) No improvement

10. Another question we often ask in those days was whether they believed in God.

(a) we will often ask (b) we are often asking

(c) we often asked (d) No improvement

11. Yes I would, if I should, rather be a sparrow than a snail.

(a) can (b) shall

(b) could (d) No improvement

12. Machines turn human society from an agrarian one into an industrial one.

(a) has turned (b) turned

(c) have turned (d) No improvement

13. I am afraid you are at cross-purpose.

(a) are at cross-purposes (b) are in cross-purposes

(c) be at cross-purposes (d) No improvement

14. I am surprised that he dares speak in such a tone to his father.

(a) he dares to speak (b) he dare to speak

(c) he dare speak (d) No improvement

15. Take care that you are not be cheated.

(a) that you will not be cheated (b) you will not be cheated

(c) that you are not cheated (d) No improvement

Exercise 24

Directions (Q. 1–15) : *Look at the underlined part of each sentence. Below each sentence are given three possible substitutions for the underlined part. If one of them (a), (b), (c) is better than the underlined part, indicate your response on the answer sheet against the corresponding letter (a), (b), (c). If none of the substitutions improves the sentence, indicate (d) as your response on the answer sheet. Thus, a 'No improvement' response will be signified by the letter (d).*

Errors may be in grammar, appropriate word usage or idioms. There may be a necessary word missing or there may be a word which should be removed.

1. He does not like me coming so late.

(a) my coming so late (b) I coming so late

(c) me come so late (d) No improvement

2. I have to cut down my expenses due to my falling income.

(a) I have to cut off (b) I have to cut out

(c) I have to cut of (d) No improvement

3. Of the two candidates, I think he is the best suited.

(a) he is suited best (b) he is the better suited

(c) he is best suited (d) No improvement

4. The climate of Delhi is somewhat like Jaipur.

(a) like Jaipur's (b) as Jaipur's

(c) as Jaipur (d) No improvement

5. His brother never has and never will be dependable.

(a) never had (b) never has been

(c) was never being (d) No improvement

6. If you would have remembered to bring the map, we would not have lost our way.

(a) had remembered (b) were remembering

(c) remembered (d) No improvement

7. You must carry on my order.

(a) carry off (b) carry out

(c) carry of (d) No improvement

8. the boat was drowned.

(a) was down (b) was drowned

(c) was sunk (d) No improvement

9. Now I must beg leave of you.

(a) beg your leave (b) beg of your leave

(c) beg off your leave (d) No improvement

10. When describing the accident, he was in tears.

(a) In describing (b) When he was describing

(c) As describing (d) No improvement

11. The two thieves distributed the loot between themselves.

(a) among themselves (b) amongst themselves

(c) with themselves (d) No improvement

12. The preservation of peace is necessary.

(a) maintenance of peace (b) establishment of peace

(c) persuasion of peace (d). No improvement

13. The spirit of democracy had sped into our way of thinking.

(a) leaked into (b) permeated

(c) soaked into (d) No improvement

14. The decent from the mountain peak was slow and painful.

(a) descent (b) decline

(c) decrease (d) No improvement

15. The building will redecorate during the summer season.

(a) will be redecorated (b) will be redecorating

(c) will be redecorate (d) No improvement

Exercise 25

***Directions (Q. 1–16)** : Look at the underlined part of each sentence. Below each sentence are given three possible substitutions for the underlined part. If one of them ,(a),(b), (c) is better than the underlined part, indicate your response in the answer sheet against the corresponding letter (a), (b), (c). If none of the substitutions improves the sentence, indicate (d) as your response on the answer sheet. Thus, a 'No improvement' response will be signified by the letter (d).*

Errors may be in grammar, appropriate word usage or idioms. There may be a necessary word missing or there may be a word which should be removed.

1. The union Finance Minister has said that fresh recruitment will be restricted to one third of the vacancies that arise in the government jobs.

(a) rise (b) raise
(c) arouse (d) No improvement

2. Our armed forces are superior to those of any other country in the world.

(a) superior than (b) superior from
(c) superior over (d) No improvement

3. He secured the first position in a hundred meters race.

(a) a hundred meter race (b) hundred meter race
(c) one hundred meters race (d) No improvement

4. Working in the slums brought her in against the realities of poverty.

(a) brought her forward (b) brought her up
(c) brought her on (d) No improvement

5. I hope it's not imposing on your hospitality, but could I stay to dinner ?

(a) stay over (b) stay up to
(c) stay at (d) No improvement

6. I have dreamt all my life for owning a beautiful maroon coloured car.

(a) of owning (b) to owning
(c) at owning (d) No improvement

7. The war has had a negative impact over the economy of the country.

(a) in the economy (b) on the economy
(c) in economy (d) No improvement

8. They claimed to bring the best products and services on the doorsteps of their consumers :

(a) up to the doorsteps (b) to the doorsteps
(c) at the doorsteps (d) No improvement

9. My company has decided to go it alone rather than set up a joint venture.
(a) put up (b) deal with
(c) go along with (d) No improvement

10. The last exercise was fairly easier than I thought it would be :
(a) more (b) rather
(c) comparatively (d) No improvement

11. The Chief Manager asked me to carry on his orders immediately.
(a) carry forward (b) carry out
(c) carry with (d) No improvement

12. The profits will be dealt with among the investors.
(a) dealt in (b) dealt out
(c) dealt of (d) No improvement

13. Your advice is no different from the other friend.
(a) not different from (b) no different from that of the
(c) not different from the (d) No improvement

14. It was she, not me, who put forth the attractive proposition.
(a) she, not I, (b) her, not me,
(c) her, not I, (d) No improvement

15. His love of languages bent him towards a career as a translator.
(a) inclined him (b) twisted him
(c) directed him (d) No improvement

16. His suggestion was greeted with hoots of laugher.
(a) greeted in (b) greeted over
(c) greeted at (d) No improvement

Exercise 26

***Directions (Q. 1–15)** : Look at the underlined part of each sentence. Below each sentence are given three possible substitutions for the underlined part. If one of them (a), (b), (c) is better than the underlined part, indicate your response on the answer sheet against the corresponding letter (a), (b), (c). If none of the substitutions improve the sentence, indicate (d) as your response on the answer sheet. Thus, a 'No improvement' response will be signified by the letter (d).*

Errors may be in grammar, appropriate word usage or idioms. There may be a necessary word missing or there may be a word which should be removed.

1. The tension between us has eased a little.
(a) eased off (b) eased up
(c) eased over (d) No improvement

2. Whenever my students come across new words, I ask them to look for them in the dictionary.

(a) to look it up (b) to look them up
(c) to look at them (d) No improvement

3. The company goes to great lengths to ensure that employees can be comfortable in their work environment.

(a) should enjoy comfort (b) will be comfortable
(c) are comfortable (d) No improvement

4. If you are living near a market you should be ready to bear the disturbances caused by traffic.

(a) to bear upon (b) to bear with
(c) to bear in (d) No improvement

5. He insisted on he was innocent.

(a) insistent on that (b) insisted that
(c) insisted with (d) No improvement

6. The child shouted that he might attract attention.

(a) to attract attention (b) in attracting attention
(c) that he may attract attention (d) No improvement

7. Each furniture on display in this hall is on sale.

(a) Each of the furniture (b) Each piece of furniture
(c) Each one of the furniture (d) No improvement

8. You must atone with your sins before you expect any pardon.

(a) atone at (b) atone to
(c) atone for (d) No improvement

9. Gangs of youth went at the rampage in the city yesterday.

(a) with the rampage (b) on the rampage
(c) over the rampage (d) No improvement

10. The whole family rallied round when mother was ill.

(a) rallied over (b) rallied at
(c) rallied with (d) No improvement

11. The building is a prime example of 1960 architecture.

(a) primary (b) paramount
(c) primitive (d) No improvement

12. Bogus social workers have been preying over old people living alone.

(a) preying with
(b) preying at
(c) preying on
(d) No improvement

13. The negotiations will call for considerable dexterity.

(a) will call considerable
(b) will call at considerable
(c) will call with considerable
(d) No improvement

14. Looked over from that point of view, his decision is easier to understand.

(a) Looked with
(b) Looked at
(c) Looked
(d) No improvement

15. He showed a flagrant disregard for anyone else's feelings.

(a) disregard at
(b) disregard over
(c) disregard with
(d) No improvement

Exercise 27

Directions (Q. 1–6) : *Look at the underlined part of each sentence. Below each sentence are given three possible substitutions for the underlined part. If one of them (a), (b), (c) is better than the underlined part, indicate your response against the corresponding letter (a), (b), (c). If none of the substitutions improves the sentence, indicate (d) as your response. Thus, a 'No improvement' response will be signified by the letter (d).*

1. The news is certainly too good to have been true.

(a) to be true
(b) to become true
(c) having been true
(d) No improvement

2. Why not Jabeen is going for his course ?

(a) Jabeen is not going
(b) is Jabeen not going
(c) Jabeen does not go
(d) No improvement

3. If I will get an opportunity, I shall attend the conference without fail.

(a) shall get
(b) get
(c) got
(d) No improvement

4. No sooner he had arrived home than he was asked to start on another journey.

(a) has he arrived
(b) he has arrived
(c) had he arrived
(d) No improvement

5. To worship idols has been our custom from times immemorial.

(a) since time
(b) for times
(c) for time
(d) No improvement

6. He quickly ordered the boy to being brought before him.
   (a) to have brought (b) to be brought
   (c) has been brought (d) No improvement

Exercise 28

***Directions (Q. 1-6) :** Look at the underlined part of each sentence. Below each sentence are given three possible substitutions for the underlined part. If one of them (a), (b), (c) is better than the underlined part, indicate your response against the corresponding letter (a), (b), (c). If none of the substitutions improves the sentence, indicate (d) as your response. Thus, a 'No improvement' response will be signified by the letter (d).*

1. He was not so good at doing sums at school as I was.
   (a) for (b) with
   (c) in (d) No improvement

2. The teacher was unhappy to find that the boy had lied rather than telling the truth.
   (a) rather than tell (b) instead of telling
   (c) rather than told (d) No improvement

3. I have seen the movie yesterday.
   (a) saw (b) had seen
   (c) was seeing (d) No improvement

4. One should be particular when he is crossing a busy lane.
   (a) he should be (b) one is
   (c) he will be (d) No improvement

5. We spoke about this yesterday, haven't we?
   (a) isn't it? (b) hadn't we?
   (c) didn't we? (d) No improvement

6. The technician and not the three managers are running the company.
   (a) were running (b) is running
   (c) have been running (d) No improvement

Exercise 29

***Directions (Q. 1–6) :** In the following questions, look at the underlined part of each sentence. Below each sentence are given three possible substitutions for the underlined part. If one of them (a), (b), (c) is better than the underlined part, indicate your response on the answer sheet against the corresponding letter (a), (b) or (c). If none of the substitutions improves the sentence, indicate (d) as your response on the answer sheet. Thus, a 'No improvement' response will be signified by the letter (d).*

1. It was not long for I discovered that the man could neither read nor write.

(a) long before (b) long since
(c) longer than (d) No improvement

2. The death toll in the cyclone went to five hundred.

(a) increased to (b) rose to
(c) spread to (d) No improvement

3. While walking on the road, a dog bit the man.

(a) a dog had bitten the man (b) the man was dogged
(c) the man was bitten by a dog (d) No improvement

4. He promised that he will deliver the goods within a week but he did not keep his promise.

(a) must have delivered (b) will have delivered
(c) would deliver (d) No improvement

5. The negotiations faced a predicament with neither side ready to offer any concession to the other.

(a) problem (b) dilemma
(c) situation (d) No improvement

6. I got up early so that I could cover most of the distance before noon.

(a) would (b) may
(c) ought (d) No improvement

Exercise 30

Directions (Q. 1–6) : *Look at the underlined part of each sentence. Below each sentence are given three possible substitutions for the underlined part. If one of them (a), (b), (c) is better than the underlined part, indicate your response against the corresponding letter (a), (b), (c). If none of the substitutions improves the sentence, indicate (d) as your response. Thus, a 'No improvement' response will be signified by the letter (d).*

1. He does not smoke, nor he drinks.

(a) nor he does drink (b) neither he does drink
(c) nor does he drink (d) No improvement

2. The patient could have been saved if he had been taken to the hospital in time.

(a) could be saved (b) could save
(c) had been saved (d) No improvement

3. I must speak to the landlord about the people above. They make much noise.

(a) much of noise (b) very much noise

(c) too much noise (d) No improvement

4. When the bomb went off, broke all of our windows.

(a) all our windows (b) all windows of us

(c) our all windows (d) No improvement

5. Knowing very little English, it was difficult to converse with the foreigner.

(a) I found it difficult to converse

(b) to converse was difficult

(c) conversing was difficult

(d) No improvement

6. He is quite well now, except a slight cold.

(a) except with a slight cold (b) excepting a slight cold

(c) except have a slight cold (d) No improvement

Exercise 31

***Directions (Q. 1–6)** : Look at the underlined part of each sentence. Below each sentence are given three possible substitutions for the underlined part. If one of them (a), (b), (c) is better than the underlined part, indicate your response against the corresponding letter (a), (b), (c). If none of the substitutions improves the sentence, indicate (d) as your response. Thus, a 'No improvement' response will be signified by the letter (d).*

1. The father together with his sons and daughters have gone to see a film.

(a) are gone (b) has gone

(c) is gone (d) No improvement

2. The stranger asked the little girl what is her name.

(a) what her name is (b) what her name was

(c) what was her name (d) No improvement

3. The family has changed house during the last six months.

(a) since the past (b) after the past

(c) for the last (d) No improvement

4. The plants are dying for the lack of water.

(a) of the lack of water (b) for lack of water

(c) out of lack of water (d) No improvement

5. The higher you climb a Himalayan peak, more cold you feel.

(a) the colder (b) the most cold

(c) colder (d) No improvement

6. If you are a resident of Agra, you might be knowing all about Ambar.

(a) would be knowing (b) might know

(c) are knowing (d) No improvement

Exercise 32

***Directions (Q. 1–6)** : Look at the underlined part of each sentence. Below each sentence are given three possible substitutions for the underlined part. If one of them (a), (b), (c) is better than the underlined part, indicate your response against the corresponding letter (a), (b), (c). If none of the substitutions improves the sentence, indicate (d) as your response. Thus, a 'No improvement' response will be signified by the letter (d).*

1. It is well- acclaimed principle that one should hold fast to his beliefs.

(a) hold fast to others beliefs (b) hold fast to their beliefs

(c) hold fast to the beliefs (d) No improvement

2. This was my business to cross the bridge, to explore the bridge head and to find out the extent to which the enemy had advanced.

(a) how much (b) the extent where

(c) the point where (d) No improvement

3. The world is becoming increasingly polarized between the rich and the poor.

(a) among rich (b) around the rich

(c) in between the rich (d) No improvement

4. I laid all the facts before him so that he could make his own judgement.

(a) laid all the facts in front of him (b) lay all the facts before him

(c) lay all the facts in front of him (d) No improvement

5. If only she had told me about her problem, I would have helped her.

(a) would help (b) could help

(c) had helped (d) No improvement

6. Apollo was worshipped as long as the Roman Empire continued.

(a) was continued (b) ruled

(c) lasted (d) No improvement

ANSWERS

Exercise 1

1. (d)	**2.** (b)	**3.** (c)	**4.** (a)	**5.** (b)

Exercise 2

1. (c)	**2.** (a)	**3.** (a)	**4.** (d)	**5.** (b)

Exercise 3

1. (b)	**2.** (d)	**3.** (c)	**4.** (e)	**5.** (a)

Exercise 4

1. (a)	**2.** (c)	**3.** (d)	**4.** (b)	**5.** (c)
6. (a)	**7.** (a)	**8.** (c)	**9.** (b)	**10.** (d)

Exercise 5

1. (a)	**2.** (a)	**3.** (b)	**4.** (a)	**5.** (c)
6. (b)	**7.** (a)	**8.** (d)	**9.** (c)	**10.** (b)

Exercise 6

1. (c)	**2.** (b)	**3.** (d)	**4.** (e)	**5.** (c)
6. (b)	**7.** (a)			

Exercise 7

1. (e)	**2.** (e)	**3.** (b)	**4.** (c)	**5.** (d)
6. (a)	**7.** (a)	**8.** (c)	**9.** (e)	**10.** (b)

Exercise 8

1. (c)	**2.** (a)	**3.** (c)	**4.** (c)	**5.** (a)
6. (d)	**7.** (b)	**8.** (a)	**9.** (b)	**10.** (a)
11. (b)	**12.** (d)	**13.** (c)	**14.** (c)	**15.** (a)

Exercise 9

1. (a)	**2.** (d)	**3.** (a)	**4.** (d)	**5.** (a)
6. (c)				

Exercise 10

1. (a)	**2.** (d)	**3.** (b)	**4.** (e)	**5.** (e)
6. (c)	**7.** (c)	**8.** (d)	**9.** (b)	**10.** (a)

Exercise 11

1. (c) **2.**(b) **3.** (e) **4.** (e) **5.** (a)
6. (b) **7.** (b) **8.** (c) **9.** (a) **10.** (d)

Exercise 12

1. (c) **2.** (d) **3.** (b) **4.** (a) **5.** (a)
6. (b) **7.** (d) **8.** (b) **9.** (b) **10.** (d)
11. (c) **12.** (a) **13.** (d) **14.** (b) **15.** (b)

Exercise 13

1. (a) **2.** (d) **3.** (b) **4.** (b) **5.** (b)
6. (d) **7.** (b) **8.** (d) **9.** (b) **10.** (a)
11. (c)

Exercise 14

1. (c) **2.** (a) **3.** (b) **4.** (d) **5.** (c)
6. (c) **7.** (c)

Exercise 15

1. (a) **2.** (c) **3.** (c) **4.** (c) **5.** (c)
6. (d)

Exercise 16

1. (c) **2.** (b) **3.** (a) **4.** (b) **5.** (b)
6. (d) **7.** (b) **8.** (a)

Exercise 17

1. (a) **2.** (c) **3.** (b) **4.** (c) **5.** (c)

Exercise 18

1. (a) **2.** (b) **3.** (a) **4.** (b) **5.** (c)
6. (d) **7.** (b) **8.** (d) **9.** (a) **10.** (b)

Exercise 19

1. (a) **2.** (b) **3.** (a) **4.** (c) **5.** (a)
6. (b) **7.** (a) **8.** (d) **9.** (c) **10.** (b)
11. (a) **12.** (c) **13.** (b) **14.** (c) **15.** (a)

Exercise 20

1. (c)	**2.** (b)	**3.** (c)	**4.** (c)	**5.** (a)
6. (c)	**7.** (b)	**8.** (c)	**9.** (a)	**10.** (c)
11. (b)	**12.** (c)	**13.** (b)	**14.** (b)	**15.** (c)

Exercise 21

1. (c)	**2.** (d)	**3.** (b)	**4.** (d)	**5.** (a)
6. (b)	**7.** (a)	**8.** (b)	**9.** (b)	**10.** (d)
11. (c)	**12.** (a)	**13.** (c)	**14.** (b)	**15.** (b)

Exercise 22

1. (c)	**2.** (c)	**3.** (b)	**4.** (d)	**5.** (a)
6. (b)	**7.** (c)	**8.** (c)	**9.** (b)	**10.** (c)
11. (b)	**12.** (c)	**13.** (b)	**14.** (c)	**15.** (d)

Exercise 23

1. (a)	**2.** (c)	**3.** (c)	**4.** (d)	**5.** (b)
6. (d)	**7.** (a)	**8.** (c)	**9.** (d)	**10.** (c)
11. (c)	**12.** (c)	**13.** (a)	**14.** (a)	**15.** (c)

Exercise 24

1. (a)	**2.** (d)	**3.** (b)	**4.** (a)	**5.** (b)
6. (a)	**7.** (b)	**8.** (c)	**9.** (d)	**10.** (b)
11. (d)	**12.** (a)	**13.** (b)	**14.** (a)	**15.** (a)

Exercise 25

1. (d)	**2.** (d)	**3.** (a)	**4.** (b)	**5.** (d)
6. (a)	**7.** (b)	**8.** (c)	**9.** (d)	**10.** (c)
11. (b)	**12.** (b)	**13.** (b)	**14.** (a)	**15.** (a)
16. (d)				

Exercise 26

1. (b)	**2.** (b)	**3.** (c)	**4.** (b)	**5.** (b)
6. (a)	**7.** (b)	**8.** (c)	**9.** (b)	**10.** (d)
11. (d)	**12.** (c)	**13.** (d)	**14.** (b)	**15.** (d)

Exercise 27

1. (a)	**2.** (b)	**3.** (b)	**4.** (c)	**5.** (a)
6. (b)				

Exercise 28

1. (d) **2.** (d) **3.** (a) **4.** (b) **5.** (c)
6. (b)

Exercise 29

1. (a) **2.** (a) **3.** (c) **4.** (c) **5.** (d)
6. (d)

Exercise 30

1. (d) **2.** (a) **3.** (c) **4.** (a) **5.** (a)
6. (c)

Exercise 31

1. (b) **2.** (b) **3.** (c) **4.** (b) **5.** (a)
6. (a)

Exercise 32

1. (d) **2.** (c) **3.** (c) **4.** (d) **5.** (d)
6. (c)